PUBLISHING STORY COLLECTIONS AND ANTHOLOGIES

by Rayne Hall

PUBLISHING STORY COLLECTIONS AND ANTHOLOGIES

by Rayne Hall

Book cover by Erica Syverson and Manuel Berbin

British English.

TABLE OF CONTENTS

INTRODUCTION

Do you want to showcase your stories in a book? Do you want to become an anthology editor and select other authors' short works? Does your writers' group plan a publication for its members?

In this book, I'll show you the professional way of publishing a collection of short tales, how to choose, organise, edit and present them, how to reach audiences and persuade readers to buy this book.

You'll learn:

- How to find fantastic stories

- Which themes have the greatest potential for success

- Creating guidelines for contributors

- How to select the right submissions

- Phrasing rejections and acceptances

- How to structure the contents, which tale to place at the start and which at the end

- Editing techniques

- How to use teasers to hook readers

- If, when and how much to pay the contributors

- What to put into the publishing agreements

- Pitfalls to avoid

- How to secure book reviews, guest post slots and social media attention and much more, taking your project to a professional level.

We'll look at the best ways to present a book showcasing your writers' group, and how to publish an anthology to raise funds for a charity.

Is a collection the same as an anthology? 'Collection' is a broad category which includes 'anthology'. If you gather several stories in a book, it's a collection, regardless of the number of authors involved. Only if the stories are by multiple authors is it an anthology. So, an anthology is a collection, but not every collection is an anthology.

While most chapters in this guide apply to either, some equip you with the specific skills you need as an anthology editor.

I'm using British English. The spelling, grammar and punctuation differ from American English, and even some words vary, but I'm sure you'll understand the content.

I've worked in publishing for forty years, and during this time I've edited many anthologies – some in the employ of publishing houses, others for my own business, Rayne Hall Ltd – and have also produced collections of my own works. I'm sharing my knowledge so you can learn from my experience, sidestep the pitfalls and avoid my mistakes.

Now let's start planning your anthology – or your single-author collection – so that you will enjoy the process and the book will become a success.

Rayne Hall

CHAPTER 1

SINGLE-AUTHOR COLLECTION OR ANTHOLOGY?

First, choose what kind of book you want to create: a collection of your own stories, or an anthology containing tales by several authors? Here are some thoughts to help you decide.

IS YOUR PROJECT A SINGLE-AUTHOR COLLECTION?

If you answer 'yes' to most of the following questions, aim for a book with your own stories.

- Do you want to showcase your own writing, provide your existing fans with another book, or attract new readers to your fiction?

- Do you have enough stories to fill a book?

- Are the stories you have in hand all in the same genre (e.g. Romance, Mystery, or Science Fiction?) or at least in closely related stories, e.g. Mystery and Thriller, Fantasy and Science Fiction?

- If you don't have enough stories in the same genre, do you have ideas for more stories, maybe even unfinished drafts you can complete?

- Are you either already established as an author in this genre, or are you seeking to become known in this genre?

IS YOUR PROJECT A MULTI-AUTHOR ANTHOLOGY?

If your answer 'yes' to most of the following questions, you're ready to start creating an anthology.

- Are you knowledgeable about the chosen genre?

- Do you want to establish yourself as an editor of anthologies?

- Do you want to help a group of writers – perhaps members of your local writers' group – to get published and showcase their writings?

- Are you networked with other writers in your genre, and do you enjoy working with them?

- Are you a good judge of writing quality?

- Are you highly organised and patient?

- Do you have a budget for paying contributors?

- Do you have the time to read and evaluate submissions?

- Are you willing to write an interesting introduction?

NOVICE MISTAKE TO AVOID

Don't produce a book containing mostly your own stories, padded out with other writers' works. This comes across as unprofessional, and can be seen as desperate. (You can, however, include your own work, as long as it doesn't dominate the book. So, if other authors have one story, you also have one. If others have three stories, you can have three.)

STRATEGY FOR SUCCESS

Think long-term. If this book is successful, can you turn it into a series?

ASSIGNMENT

1. Choose whether you want to publish an anthology of multiple authors' works, or a collection with only your own stories.

2. Visit a bookselling website, and browse short story collections in your chosen genre – either single-author collections or anthologies, whichever you've chosen. Look especially at books published in the past three years which are selling well. Read their blurbs (descriptions), their free sample pages, and the reviews they've received from readers. This will give you a good idea of the market and what readers want.

CHAPTER 2

CHOOSING THE GENRE AND THE THEME

To lay the groundwork for your book's success, think about its content. The formula is simple: single genre – single form – single theme.

STICK TO ONE GENRE

Short story collections sell best if they focus on one genre, for example, Romance, Fantasy, Historical, Science Fiction or Horror. Collections within a sub-genre have even greater marketing potential, e.g. Paranormal Romance, Urban Fantasy, Mediaeval Historical, Dystopian Science Fiction or Psychological Horror.

This is because most readers look for their next read in their favourite genre. Rather than browsing thousands of published short story collections, they go straight to the 'Romance' category, or type 'Paranormal Romance stories' in the search box.

So if you write both Romance and Horror stories, don't put them in the same book.

Professional Tip: collections within sub-genres – or even sub-sub-genres – have the best chance of getting discovered by readers.

DECIDE ON THE FORM

Choose what forms of writing your book will contain: short stories, non-fiction (essays and articles), or poems? In this guide, we're looking at short story collections, but you could opt for a different form. Just don't mix it all up, because readers buying a book to read articles don't usually want to see poetry, and short story lovers would get frustrated to find essays and articles.

Stick to short stories (or, if you prefer, to non-fiction or poetry). This will make it easier to get sales.

Professional tip: use the book's subtitle to clarify what kind of writing the book contains, e.g. *Twelve Tales of Murder and Mystery* or *Stories for the Summer Season.*

CHOOSE A THEME

Story collections with a theme sell much better than those without one. A theme could be, for example: Seaside, Mother's Day, Italy or Animal Rescue.

Readers love stories about their favourite subjects. People who are passionate about pets will be drawn to a book with stories of animal rescues, while readers with fond memories of Italy will reach for the collection of stories set in that country. Themed story collections are also popular as gift books: "What can we give Suzie for her birthday? She's a bookworm and loves the seaside. Let's get her a book with seaside stories!"

Seasonal themes can work well. You could create a collection of stories about Valentine's Day, Easter, Mother's Day, Christmas, Hanukkah, Eid, Beltane or Halloween.

Professional Tip: check the competition. Every year, so many new books with Christmas stories get published that it can be difficult for yours to stand out, whereas Beltane or Easter are relatively rare.

NOVICE MISTAKES TO AVOID

You may yearn to publish a book showcasing the broad spectrum of your writing, but unless you're famous, strangers won't be interested enough to spend their money or time on this. Be professional and assess rationally which part of your writing will work best.

First-time publishers often want to publish their friends' writings, but this project is doomed if each friend writes something different.

A children's story, a gruesome horror tale, a philosophical poem and a historical essay may each be great – but they don't belong together in one book. Sometimes you need to compromise and allow a mix of genres, of forms or of themes – but you should never compromise on all three and publish an unfocused hotchpotch.

MISTAKES I MADE AND LEARNT FROM

When I created the Ten Tales anthology series, I wanted to include both Fantasy and Horror stories, largely because I had friends who wrote in those genres. I reasoned that Fantasy and Horror are related genres, and that fans of one would probably also enjoy the other.

Although it worked to a degree, I realise now why real success eluded us: Fantasy fans preferred Fantasy books, and Horror fans Horror. While they were willing to read a story outside their genre now and then, they didn't want to spend money on it. I should have focused on either Fantasy or Horror fiction.

These days, I give my anthologies a much tighter focus. For example, *Among the Headstones: Creepy Tales from the Graveyard* contains Horror stories – and more specifically, Gothic Horror which is more creepy than gory. Some of the stories have Fantasy elements, and that's fine as long as they fit into the category of Gothic Horror.

PROFESSIONAL STRATEGY

The tighter the focus of genre, form and theme, the greater is the book's marketing potential.

ASSIGNMENT

Choose the genre, form and theme for your book. Discuss your ideas with readers of the genre, and in the case of an anthology, with some of the writers you hope will contribute.

CHAPTER 3

HOW MANY STORIES DO YOU NEED?

You can collect as many or as few stories as you like. There are no rules. However, you must not disappoint your readers.

The trend is for bigger books. In the early years of ebooks, publishers brought out collections of just three or four stories, and readers purchased them. Nowadays, readers expect to get more stories for their money, and books with under eight scarcely stand a chance. Ten to twenty is better. Some anthologies, especially in the ebook format, contain fifty or more stories.

However, there are other considerations. If your stories are long – say, over 10,000 words each – then four or five can fill a book. On the other hand, if you're gathering flash fiction pieces shorter than 1,000 words, you'll need to offer twenty-five as a minimum.

CHOOSE THE TITLE TO MANAGE EXPECTATIONS

Don't raise false expectations. Use the title or subtitle to tell readers how much they'll get. For example:

Daring to Dance: A Dozen Dirty Stories

Daring to Dance: Twenty Tales of Sizzling Splendour

Daring to Dance: Thirteen Sizzling Stories

The Big Book of Sizzling Erotic Tales

The Mammoth Book of Hot Dance Stories

Whatever your title promises – whether that's a specific number or an implied quantity – the book has to deliver. If you call your anthology The *Mammoth Book of Mystery Stories,* readers will be disappointed if they get fewer than fifty tales. *The Collected Steampunk Stories of Suzie Scrybe* implies a sizeable collection, probably at least a dozen, and readers will feel cheated if they get only three.

However, if it's intended as a series, it's best not to name specific numbers, because trends may change.

Unfortunately, some readers have unrealistic expectations outside our control. Years ago, my book *Six Scary Tales* received a negative review by a reader who complained, "What a rip-off! This book contains only six stories."

NOVICE MISTAKE TO AVOID

Don't pad your book with below-standard or thematically irrelevant content just to get the word count up.

PROFESSIONAL STRATEGY

Think in advance about how many stories you want, and in what word count range. You don't need to decide the precise number, but you need a clear idea.

For example, for a single-author collection you might say, "I want my collection to be about 40,000 words long. I already have fifteen stories, on average 2,000 words long." This shows you that you need to write five additional tales to fill the book.

For an anthology, your assessment might look something like this: "For this book, I want about twelve stories, each between 3,000 and 7,000 words long. This will make the book about 60,000 words." This leaves the way open to adjust your plan according to the submissions you receive.

ASSIGNMENT

Look at anthologies and collections in your genre published in the past three years, especially those with high sales rankings and many reviews. How many stories do they contain? Use this as a guide for your choice.

CHAPTER 4

TITLE AND SUBTITLE

Give your book not only a title, but a subtitle. The additional words boost the reader-hooking power, and they make the book more discoverable on bookselling sites.

WHAT YOUR TITLE AND SUBTITLE NEED TO CONVEY

Use the title and subtitle to convey as much of the following as possible, either implied or spelled out:

- The genre

- The theme

- The form (e.g. stories or poems)

- (optional: a hint at the number of stories)

Here are some examples I've made up:

Love Under the Mistletoe:
The Mammoth Book of Christmas Romance Stories

Sweet Sixteen: 16 Romance Tales for that Special Birthday

The Cursed Abbey: 13 Gothic Tales of Ghostly Ruins

Dark Waves: Horror Stories of the Sea

Here are some of mine:

The Bride's Curse: Bulgarian Gothic Ghost and Horror Stories

Undead: Ten Tales of Zombies

Dragon: Ten Tales of Fiery Beasts

Among the Headstones: Creepy Tales from the Graveyard

INCLUDE THRILL WORDS

Each genre has certain words which make readers' hearts beat faster.

For example, fans of the Western genre respond to *cowboy, sheriff, Texas, posse, gun, wagon, ranch, bonanza, stagecoach, saloon, claim, ride, rustler, shooter, canyon, mustang, marshal, trail, lode, West.*

Lovers of the Regency Romance, on the other hand, take notice when they see *ball, coming out, debutante, rake, rogue, proposal, duke, viscount, scandal, wicked, heiress, eligible, betrothal, promise, count, lord, mistress, lady, trap.*

Readers who adore epic fantasy see *dragon, sword, quest, queen, treasure, magic, spell, throne, wizard, warlord, warrior, wrath.*

Thriller readers respond to *death, deadly, killer, kill, murder, crime, threat.*

For Gothic fiction, alluring words include *doom, curse, bride, secret, haunting, grave, ghost, storm.*

One or two thrill words are enough. More can come across as hackneyed.

CONSTRUCTING THE TITLE AND SUBTITLE

Although you can play around with what to put where, it usually works best if the title is relatively short (so you can place it in large letters on the cover page) and includes one of the genre's thrill words.

If you're stuck for ideas, lift one of the story titles and use it as a book title. This works especially well for single-author collections.

I used this approach for my Gothic collection *The Bride's Curse*. It's the title of one of the stories, is short, and contains two of the genre's thrill words.

The subtitle can then be more informative, containing the genre, the theme and perhaps the number of stories.

NOVICE MISTAKE TO AVOID

Don't choose a 'clever' title the meaning of which can't be immediately understood.

MISTAKES I MADE AND LEARNT FROM

When I launched a series of Fantasy/Horror anthologies, I looked for a subtitle I could adapt for all books in the series. I chose *Ten Tales of...* because I was in love with the alliteration. At the time, many anthologies were between eight and twelve stories long, so it fit.

And at first, the books performed well: *Haunted: Ten Tales of Ghosts, Bites: Ten Tales of Vampires, Fiends: Ten Tales of Demons* and so on. Then trends changed, and anthologies became longer. Ten stories just wasn't enough anymore, and sales dropped. I knew what the problem was... but I couldn't change the title, because the series was established under that name.

I wish I'd opted for a different alliteration, such as *Terrifying Tales of...*, or *Startling Stories of...*

I considered switching to *Twenty Tales of...* but that could have renewed the problem if trends changed again. I learnt my lesson: stating the number of stories in the title or subtitle is a good thing... but it's foolish to make it the brand identifier of a long-term series.

PROFESSIONAL STRATEGY

What keywords are readers of your genre looking for when they search for a book to buy? Including those in the title or subtitle will boost sales.

ASSIGNMENTS

1. Browse recently published books in your genre. What thrill words are they using in the title?

2. Come up with three or more title/subtitle ideas for your project. Run it past readers of the genre, and ask them which they prefer.

CHAPTER 5

HOW TO FIND STORIES FOR YOUR ANTHOLOGY

You need stories to fill your anthology. Finding the right stories can be a bigger challenge than you may think, requiring a lot of time and thought.

Once you've decided on the genre, theme and approximate number of stories you want, here are several routes you can take.

ASK THE WRITERS YOU KNOW

As a writer, you're probably in contact with other writers. Consider the members of your writers' circle, genre forum, writing workshop or critique group. Who writes the kind of fiction you're after? Tell them about your planned project and ask if they want to contribute a story. Many will respond with enthusiasm. Some of them already have a suitable story in need of a home. Perhaps a tale has been rejected by another publisher but would be just right for your anthology. Others have an idea or a draft which could be polished, and yet others love the challenge of creating a piece from scratch.

What not to do: be careful not to promise publication at this stage. The story may not be suitable or good enough, and you may have to reject it, which can lead to hurt feelings. Instead, simply say that you'd love to read the story and consider it for publication.

ANNOUNCE THE PROJECT IN YOUR WRITERS' GROUPS

If you're a member of a writers' group, ask the leader for permission to announce your project at the next meeting. Outline what you're looking for and invite members to contribute. If there's enough interest, you can even organise a session where members craft stories specifically for this theme.

What not to do: don't take it personally if group members don't share your enthusiasm for the project.

POST IN WRITERS' FORUMS

If you're a member of online forums, you can post your request there. The best results come from genre-specific forums, e.g. for Romance writers or Science Fiction writers, in which you've been an active participant for a while.

What not to do: when internet trolls reply to your post with nasty comments, don't get provoked into a fight.

INVITE PREVIOUS CONTRIBUTORS

If you've published anthologies before, take a note of the writers who produced great stories, were dependable and pleasant to work with, carried out revisions promptly and pulled their weight in the promotional efforts. It can be a good idea to contact these trusted writers before you spread the word elsewhere.

What not to do: don't expect your favourite writers to find out about the anthology through the grapevine. They deserve a personal invitation to submit.

ASK OTHER ANTHOLOGY EDITORS

If you know people who have published anthologies in related genres, ask them to put you in touch with their trusted writers. You can ask specifically, "I love the story by Suzie Scrybe. Her snarky style would be exactly right for an anthology I'm planning. Could you put me in touch with her, please?" or ask for suggestions. "I'm planning an anthology about XYZ-theme, and I wonder if you can recommend writers who may be interested in contributing." Editors like to help one another, and they also want to do a favour to their valued authors.

What not to do: don't behave like an entitled prat, expecting other editors' support when you've never done anything for them and haven't even read their books.

TRAWL THE INTERNET

Visit websites where writers showcase their work, such as DeviantArt.com and Wattpad.com. These sites feature many stories, and may have the type you want, though the pieces are not always of publishable quality. Draw up a list of possible stories, and approach the authors for publishing permission. To communicate with the authors, you will probably have to create an account on that site.

Critique workshops – especially genre-specific ones – contain a wealth of stories in progress. I find that the quality of material in genre-specific workshops like Critters.org (Science Fiction, Fantasy, Horror) is often high, although the authors will need time for a final revision.

Many novelists feature free short stories on their websites, as samples to entice new readers. They are often happy to have these stories included in anthologies, since this gives them more publicity. This can be a way to secure contributions by well-known writers. So trawl the websites of authors in your genre, and if you see good stories, ask if you may use them.

What not to do: don't just help yourself to stories. You need the author's written permission, otherwise this could get you into trouble for intellectual property theft and breach of copyright.

RUN A WRITING CONTEST

Announce a writing competition, where the theme is your anthology's topic, and the best story wins a prize. You may receive many entries which are exactly right for your project. However, be aware that organising a writing contest involves a lot of work.

Some contests charge an entry fee. Be careful: while this sounds like an easy way to earn money, it can open the door to a myriad of legal issues. If you want to run a fee-charging contest, consult a lawyer first.

What not to do: don't promise publication for the winning entry, because even the best submission may not be good enough to include in the book. Merely say, "The best stories will be considered for inclusion in the anthology."

INCLUDE OUT-OF-COPYRIGHT CLASSICS

When an author has been dead for more than seventy years, their work is usually out of copyright and can be published. This means you may be able to include the works of famous authors like Charles Dickens and Edgar Allan Poe in your anthology – for free.

Project Gutenberg makes many out-of-copyright literary works available to download free of charge, and you are permitted to include those in commercial projects. You can also find stories in old printed books and type them up.

Copyright rules vary from country to country. In some, the copyright expires seventy years after the author's death, in others, fifty years. This creates a 'dodgy' twenty-year period which can lead to legal problems for international publication. Personally, I err on the safe side and include only authors who've been dead for at least seventy years.

What not to do: don't use stories by living authors, or stories which may still be in copyright.

STUDY ALREADY-PUBLISHED ANTHOLOGIES AND COLLECTIONS

Read anthologies and collections in the genre, especially those with related themes. Identify the stories you'd love to have in your own book, and contact the authors via their websites or social media accounts. Tell them how much you love their tale and ask if you may feature it in your anthology. Although many authors will decline or not reply at all, others will be delighted that their story will get anthologised again.

What not to do: don't use more than three stories from the same anthology, otherwise your book may look like an imitation project.

GET YOUR PROJECT LISTED IN WRITERS' MARKETS

Websites like Duotrope.com and HorrorTree.com list publications open for submission, and they usually have a category for anthologies. Tell them the genre, the theme, the period during which you consider submissions, the rights you require, the payment you offer and your web address. This will probably yield many submissions – possibly more than you can handle.

What not to do: don't use this avenue unless you're prepared to handle a deluge of slush.

NOVICE MISTAKE TO AVOID

Don't include stories by your friends simply because they're nice people and you want to do them a favour. It's your responsibility to compile tales of the highest calibre you can get.

PROFESSIONAL STRATEGY

Don't be shy to feature one of your own tales, showcasing your skill as a fiction writer. This will increase the number of stories, and you won't have to worry about payment and copyright issues. Anthology readers may be drawn to the book by the more famous contributors, but take such delight in your yarn that they seek out more by its author. This can boost sales of your other books, increase your fan base, enhance your reputation as an author and further your career.

However, don't include more stories by you than by other writers. If each author has one story in the book, then it would look awkward if there are five by you.

ASSIGNMENT

Choose which of the outlined avenues you will explore.

CHAPTER 6

CAN ANYONE SUBMIT TO YOUR ANTHOLOGIES?

You can make your project an 'open-submission' or 'closed' anthology.

With an open-submission policy, you allow everyone to send you their stories for consideration. With a closed anthology, only authors you have personally invited may submit.

PROS AND CONS OF OPEN-SUBMISSION ANTHOLOGIES

Instead of searching for stories, you let the stories come to you. After listing it on one or several writers' market sites, you can sit back and await what comes in.

This is a good option if you don't know many writers in that genre, or if you want to consider a wide variety of submissions. Unfortunately, open-call submissions draw a lot of dross, with writers dumping anything they've written, whether it fits the purpose or not. Many people don't bother to read the guidelines, they just send anything. For the anthology *The Haunted Train: Creepy Tales from the Railways* I received many stories which didn't even feature a train or a station, or merely mentioned them in passing. I also received poetry collections, photographs and a novel trilogy.

Many submissions will be of low standard, poorly written, derivative, or churned out by AI apps. Then you have the work of sifting through the slush to find the gems, which takes more work than you might imagine. You'll need to reject the unsuitable offerings, and deal with the bruised egos of hopeful wannabes who send nasty emails, complaining that you don't understand their literary genius.

Tip: instead of publicising your personal or professional email address, create a disposable email for just this project.

PROS AND CONS OF CLOSED ANTHOLOGIES

Instead of wading through slush and dealing with unprofessional wannabes, you invite the writers whose work you value to submit a story.

An invitation isn't a promise to publish the story. You merely agree to consider it.

This is a good option if you personally know suitable writers who can pen a great story, deliver reliably and are pleasant to work with. Since I have published many anthologies, I have a 'stable' of strong, dependable contributors, and I always invite them first.

You may also invite members of your online and in-person writers' groups.

You can invite authors whom you don't personally know, but be aware that top authors expect top payment, so consider your budget.

By inviting only authors you like, you can avoid a lot of stress. However, you may not get enough stories this way. Another drawback is that a series in which every book features the same group of authors can be predictable, lacking freshness and new voices.

If a story by a personal friend is simply not good enough for inclusion, you'll face the problem of how to inform them of the rejection. True professionals will take it in their stride, but inexperienced writers may take it personally, and this can ruin friendships.

Tip: invite more writers to submit than you have slots available, because not every writer will submit, and not all submissions will come up to your expectations.

NOVICE MISTAKES TO AVOID

Writers who have suffered a lot of rejections for their own stories often get a 'power rush' when they're the ones who do the accepting and rejecting. This can lead to poor judgement as well as to unadvised interactions.

SUCCESS STRATEGY

Consider starting with a 'closed' approach. Invite the authors whose fiction and professionalism you respect to submit. If this doesn't yield the desired quantity or variety, issue an open-call to get more contributions.

ASSIGNMENTS

1. Decide whether you want to make your book an 'open-call' or a 'closed' anthology.

2. For an open-call anthology, think about where you will publicise the call – e.g. on a genre-specific market listing website. For a closed anthology, draw up a list of writers you want to invite.

CHAPTER 7

CREATE GUIDELINES FOR CONTRIBUTORS

If you plan to compile an anthology, you need to let writers know exactly what you're looking for, and what terms you are offering. Give this document to the authors you're inviting, publish it on your website, share it in writing forums.

WHAT TO INCLUDE

- **The genre, format and theme.** Examples: 'We're seeking historical short stories about strong women.' 'This anthology will feature short stories in the Extreme Horror genre'

- **The length.** Examples: 'We are looking for stories of 2,000-4,000 words.' 'The ideal length is 5,000 words, but we will consider stories which are shorter or longer'

- **The closing date.** Examples: 'Our reading period is 1 March – 30 May 2024.' 'Closing date for submissions: 18 November 2023'

- **Who is eligible?** Examples: 'We accept submissions only from members of the LGTB+ community.' 'Only residents of New Zealand are eligible to submit.' (If you have no such restrictions, you can leave this out)

- **Tone and style.** Examples: 'We seek fast-paced, exciting stories.' 'We want third-person Point-of-View stories with realistic plots'

- **What you particularly want:** 'Humorous stories are welcome.' – 'I'm especially interested in stories set in Africa'

- **What to avoid.** Examples: 'No explicit sex and no graphic violence.' 'We're not interested in vampires or werewolves'

- **Do you accept reprints (previously published pieces)?** Examples: 'Previously published stories welcome.' 'Original stories only, no reprints'

- **Do you accept multiple submissions (authors sending several stories)?** For example, 'Multiple submissions welcome.' 'Only one story per author, please'

- **Do you accept simultaneous submissions (authors send the same story to several publishers)?** For example, 'No sim subs.' 'Simultaneous submissions are OK, but notify us if the story gets accepted elsewhere'

- **What rights do you acquire?** Examples: 'We purchase first worldwide rights, exclusive for one year after publication.' 'All rights remain with the author'

- **How much you pay.** Examples: 'No pay, but contributors receive a paperback copy.' '300 US$ for original stories, 75 US$ for reprints'

- **How to format the submission.** Examples: 'Times New Roman Font, indented paragraphs.' 'Printed on one side of A4 paper with numbered pages, double spacing and wide margins'

- **How to submit.** Examples: 'Send your submission as an email attachment to Eddie.Editor@emailaddress.com.' 'Use the submission form on our website'

- **Anticipated Decision Dates**. Examples: 'We will accept or decline your story by 20 April 2024.' 'We aim to notify you of our decision before the end of the year'

- **Anticipated Publication Date.** Examples: 'The book will be published in 2025.' 'I anticipate a Halloween launch this year'

- **Editor's Name.** Examples: 'The editors are Suzie Scrybe and Eddie Torr.' 'This anthology will be edited by historical novelist Klaus Schreiber'

SAMPLE GUIDELINES

These are for a fictitious anthology I've just invented, so don't submit. You can model your own guidelines on these.

GUIDELINES FOR SUBMISSION

Cathy's Cat Care is publishing its second anthology to raise funds to help pay for veterinary treatment for injured cats.

Wanted:

Short stories about cats who get rescued, or who have been rescued.

Especially welcome

Heart-warming tales with uplifting endings. Stories in which cats also rescue humans in some way.

What we don't want

Stories depicting graphic violence against animals. Stories in which cats are portrayed as evil.

Genre

Any

Length

500-5,000 words

Reprints (previously published stories)

Yes – very welcome, provided you own the copyright

Multiple submissions
(submitting several stories to this anthology)

Yes

Simultaneous submission
(submitting to other markets at the same time)

No problem

Payment

Flat fee, 1 Euro per story, regardless of length. This is a fundraising anthology, and profits will be used to help cats in need

Rights

One-time publication rights for this anthology. The writer retains all rights to the story and can publish it elsewhere

Editors

Felix Purrer and Katinka Paws

Submission Period

2 June – 15 August 2024

Submissions:

Send entries as email attachments to editors@cathyscatcare.com.

Decisions

Selected authors will be notified before 30 November 2024, probably much earlier. If we like your story, but it's not quite right, we may ask for changes (especially in the case of previously unpublished stories). You can decide whether you want to make those changes and have the story included. Requested changes need to be made promptly.

Publication Date

We aim to launch the paperback at our annual Feline Festival in spring 2025.

NOVICE MISTAKE TO AVOID

Don't make the formatting requirements complicated. If writers have to spend a lot of time reformatting their stories with the right kind of fonts, paragraph indents, quote marks, scene breaks, page numbering, headers, footers and titles, many will not bother. Their time is precious, and they don't want to waste it if they don't even know whether the story will be included.

Frankly, you don't need this exact formatting to decide whether a story is suitable, do you? If you want to save yourself work by accepting only correctly formatted stories, you can always add the sentence, 'Accepted authors will be asked to format their stories in our house style.'

SUCCESS STRATEGY

Keep to the point, without wordy waffling, and present the requirements clearly. The tighter and clearer the Guidelines for Contributors, the more professional the submissions you receive.

ASSIGNMENT

Create Guidelines for Contributors for your anthology project.

CHAPTER 8

WHO OWNS THE RIGHTS TO THE STORIES?

The author of a story automatically owns the copyright. She can sell this right to someone else, or she can give permission for someone to publish the story.

What does this mean for you as the publisher of an anthology? You need the author's (or other copyright holder's) permission to include the piece in your book. You agree between you what this permission includes and what rights you acquire.

THE BASIC OPTIONS

'The author retains all rights.'

Also known as 'non-exclusive publishing rights', this the simplest arrangement. I choose this every time, because I feel strongly that writers, not publishers, should own the rights to their work.

The author allows you, the publisher, to publish the story in this anthology. You're not allowed to publish it elsewhere or to sell it to another publisher. The author can also publish the story elsewhere, e.g. on a website, in a single-author collection, or in another anthology.

I recommend this option if you want to keep things simple, if you want to include previously-published pieces, and also if you plan to pay the authors little or nothing.

'First Rights.'

With this arrangement, the author allows you to publish a brand new story before anyone else does. This allows you to promote your anthology as containing 'brand new stories, never before published'.

The author keeps all other rights, and can submit the story elsewhere as soon as your anthology is published. So although you were the first to publish it, it may be published elsewhere a few days later, and even available for free on the internet, destroying your marketing advantage.

If you're interested in this option, I recommend that you consider 'First Rights with Exclusivity Period' instead.

'First Rights with Exclusivity Period.'

This is similar to the previous option: you are the first to publish his story. However, the author has to wait a certain period (usually one year) after publication before publishing the story elsewhere. This helps with the marketing, because for the first year of publication, you can say that the book contains tales not published anywhere else.

Be aware that First Rights are valuable, and authors expect to be paid accordingly. If you want First Rights – with or without exclusivity – be prepared to pay professional or at least semi-professional rates.

Although the exclusivity clause is perfectly reasonable (if you pay for the privilege), authors are wary. If the anthology gets postponed repeatedly, or never gets published, then the story is in limbo and can never get published anywhere. For the author of a great story, this is a painful situation.

I recommend inserting a clause in the contract: 'If the anthology is not published by [date, perhaps two years after the signature], all rights automatically revert to the author.' This removes the stress and worry.

'First Rights with Exclusivity Period' is a good option to choose if you have a substantial budget and grand plans for the book.

It's not suitable if you want to include previously published stories, for an amateur project, or if you want to pay the contributors nothing or only a token fee.

'Publisher Owns All Rights.'

The writer signs over the copyright to you. You can now do with the story whatever you like – publish it, bury it, sell it to someone else. The writer, on the other hand, may not publish the story anywhere else.

Asking a writer to relinquish All Rights is drastic. Do this only if you're prepared to pay serious money.

OBSOLETE TERMS

In the past, authors granted rights for certain geographic regions, and besides 'first rights' there were second, third, fourth rights and so on. Writers were selling 'First British Serial Rights' and 'Second North American Serial Rights'.

In the days of international publication and electronic publishing, these terms have become obsolete. You may still see them here or there, but I advise you not to use them for your project.

NOVICE MISTAKES TO AVOID

Don't just use a story you've found in a book or on the internet. You need the author's permission, otherwise you're committing intellectual property theft, which is a serious crime.

Don't neglect to spell out what rights you acquire, and put it in writing. Misunderstandings could lead to arguments and legal complications.

STRATEGY FOR SUCCESS

Choose 'Author Retains all Rights' – this is clear, simple, avoids conflict, costs little, allows you to include reprints, and makes the authors happy.

The other option worth considering is 'First Rights with Exclusivity Period.' I wouldn't advise any of the others.

FROM MY PERSONAL EXPERIENCE

I'm always generous with the rights: I only ask for permission to include the stories in my book, and the authors keep all rights. Most writers are relieved and grateful when they see this, and happy to let me publish their tales.

One writer refused to sign the contract unless I inserted a 'rights reversal' clause. 'If the book is not published by such-and-such date, the rights automatically revert to the author.' Such a clause is sensible in case of 'First Rights with Exclusivity' but here it made no sense whatsoever. Since the author already owned all rights, there were no rights to revert. I explained this to her, but she remained belligerent: either I inserted the (pointless) clause in the contract, or she would not sign.

I deduced that this writer just wanted to feel important and assert power over the publisher – not a good attitude in a business relationship. I thanked her for submitting and declined the story.

ASSIGNMENT

Decide which of the four options is right for your project.

CHAPTER 9

PAYING THE WRITERS

If you publish an anthology, you normally pay the writers for the use of their stories. This is a delicate and often confusing issue, so here are some guidelines.

DO YOU ALWAYS NEED TO OFFER PAYMENT?

Not necessarily. You can state upfront that this is a 'for the luv' project, and nobody gets paid.

Many writers, especially those at the beginning of their writing career, are happy to see their stories published in a nice book. More experienced authors often agree to have previously published stories reprinted in anthologies, because it's a way for them to get their work discovered by new readers and to become better known in the genre. Writers' groups showcasing members' works don't normally pay, and fundraising anthologies are often non-paying as well.

WHY YOU SHOULD OFFER PAYMENT

The higher the pay, the higher the quality of the submissions. Only amateurs and novices write 'for the luv' – and their stories are on average not so great. Professionals and semi-pros won't submit to non-paying markets (though they may make exceptions for fundraising projects, or they may let you have a previously published story).

If you want First Rights to stories, you definitely need to be prepared to pay.

HOW PAYMENT IS CALCULATED

You can either offer a 'flat fee' i.e. a fixed amount per story, or you can pay per word.

Stay away from the 'royalties' arrangement where contributors earn a share of the book's income or profit. This payment model works for novels, but isn't suitable for anthologies, and only leads to never-ending accounting work, stress and conflict.

PAYMENT RATES EXPLAINED

Pay Per Word

Writers get paid depending on how long their story is, either per word or per 1,000 words.

Flat Fee Per Story

Each story receives the same payment, regardless of length.

Reprint Fee

If you include both previously published and never-before published stories, then you can offer a lower fee for the previously published ones.

Professional Rates

Top anthologies pay top rates for top stories. The rates are usually stated per word. Look up what currently counts as 'professional rate' in that genre – it may be a minimum 0.08 US$ per word. Prestigious anthologies pay much more. If you want your anthology to be among the finest published that year and have the budget, you can attract high-class writers to your project.

Semi-professional Rates

These attract mostly writers who are established in their genre and can craft superb stories, but are not famous. 0.01 US$ per word is considered the minimum in the semi-professional range.

Token

If you can't afford to pay much, but are paying something, that's called a 'token' payment. For example, you may offer 5 or 10 US$ per story. This will attract better quality submissions than 'for the luv', because the writers feel that their work is valued. Token-paying anthologies also attract submissions of previously published high-quality works.

For the Luv

These are non-paying anthologies. The contributors are amateurs who love writing and enjoy the thrill of seeing their work published.

Treat the writers with respect and thank them for their generous permission to use the story. You may not be able to pay, but you can give appreciation. Send each contributor a free copy – at least of the ebook, which costs you nothing.

Exposure

Some publishers say: 'We pay in exposure.' This means, the writers should be grateful to be included, and they will get nothing, not even a book. This is an arrogant, disrespectful attitude.

'Exposure' anthologies are frowned upon in the publishing world. Exposure isn't payment; it's what writers get paid for. If you pretend that you're doing writers a favour, it shows that you're not respecting them. This will quickly cost you the respect of your peers in the genre. The submissions you'll receive are those of writers who are desperate to get published because their stories aren't good enough to stand a chance elsewhere.

Reading Fees and Paid Publication

Some publishers, observing that there are more writers seeking to get published in anthologies than there are anthologies seeking writers, have hit upon the idea to exploit naïve writers.

Instead of paying for permission to include stories, they charge for publication. Some even charge 'reading fees' to look at submissions.

These anthologies rarely sell, because the content is of low quality, penned by wannabes who haven't mastered the storytelling craft.

This unethical business model will get you blackballed in the writing and publishing community and may destroy your career prospects as a writer or editor.

Don't even think about stooping so low.

WHEN AND HOW TO PAY

You should commit in the contract to pay 'on publication' i.e. when the book is published. Don't keep the writers waiting, but send the payment immediately, or at least within a month.

If all contributors reside in the same country, payments can be made easily by bank transfer. For international payments, the bank transfer fees are prohibitive, so you need to use an international payment platform.

Getting everyone's bank details and filling in forms can take up far more time than you imagine, especially for international payments. I confess that I find the sorting out of payments the most stressful part of publishing an anthology.

FROM MY PERSONAL EXPERIENCE

In the early days of ebooks, I published 'for the luv' anthologies. I didn't get a lot of submissions and had to search for publishable pieces. When I altered my strategy and offered a token of 1US$ per story, the quality of stories immediately improved. I realised that there's a big psychological difference between 'for the luv' and 'token' payments. For new writers, it feels great to be paid for their writing, even if it's just one dollar.

The anthologies I'm currently publishing are mostly token-paying markets. I offer a flat fee of 10 Euro, regardless of story length and previous publication. I get fine submissions by new voices (for whom this is their first ever publication success) and also many fantastic previously published stories by experienced authors.

What I hate is when writers submit stories, and when chosen, they demand to be paid more than everyone else. They've read the Guidelines for Contributors and knew how much (or how little) I could pay – but feel entitled to more. Some have the nerve to claim that they are worth more than other writers. No way. I'm not in the business of feeding inflated egos. In such situations, I don't even argue – I simply say, "Thank you for submitting. Good luck in placing your story elsewhere." Then I pick another story to fill that slot.

NOVICE MISTAKE TO AVOID

Don't make payment dependent on crowdfunding. Crowdfunding campaigns for anthologies by unknown editors rarely raise much, if anything. The attempt will mark you as inexperienced and unprofessional.

Better state upfront that this is a 'for the luv' project.

STRATEGY FOR SUCCESS

Whatever you decide regarding payments, state the payment (or non-payment) upfront, so writers can decide if they wish to submit on those terms.

Be consistent and offer all contributors the same terms.

ASSIGNMENT

Decide if and how much you are going to pay your contributors.

CHAPTER 10

SELECTING STORIES

Choose stories on three main criteria: relevance, quality and variety. For a single-author collection, this is straightforward. But if you're publishing an anthology, you may deal with dozens, hundreds and perhaps thousands of submissions.

START BY SIFTING OUT THE DROSS

I've learnt from experience that the best approach is to start by eliminating the unsuitable stories. A large number of submissions are simply not right for this book. Discard those, and you'll see clearly what your real choices are.

I recommend that you eliminate the following right away:

- **The wrong form.** When you ask for short stories, some people send poems, articles and whole books. You don't even need to read those to know they're wrong

- **The wrong genre.** For example, you want Historical stories and the writers send Science Fiction. However, I recommend that you keep submissions which straddle genres, e.g. Historical Romance

- **Not about the theme.** Surprisingly many submissions don't interpret the theme. The writers simply send any story, merely inserting a brief mention. For example, if your anthology is about weddings, they sent a story about a birthday party and replace the word 'birthday' with 'wedding'. Or they insert a dialogue line where a character mentions that she'll soon be a bride. Be strict: if the story doesn't revolve around the theme, it's out

In addition, here are two further criteria I use for discarding stories at this stage:

- **Immature writing voice.** New writers use the following words a lot: look, turn, could, start, begin, shrug, smile, sigh. As a result, their voices sound the same, and in an anthology, this would be dull. Also, if they haven't developed their authentic voice yet, chances are they haven't mastered the art of plotting a great story either. Thus, if the first page of a manuscript is crammed with sighs, smiles, looks and turns, I know that this submission isn't up to the high standard I seek. You may decide to be more lenient about this, especially if you're editing a 'for the luv' project or showcasing members of a beginner writers' group

- **Problem authors.** Like many experienced anthology editors, I keep a list of writers whom I will not consider again. These include those who promised to send revised versions and didn't, who responded to rejection with rants and insults, and who were acting like prima donnas expecting star treatment and better pay than the others. I simply don't want to go through that again. My list also contains writers whom I've observed behaving badly on social media, e.g. picking fights, trolling or insulting those of different faiths. I don't want this sort of behaviour associated with the Rayne Hall author brand

I suggest you let these authors know immediately that you will not be publishing their stories. You'll find a sample rejection letter in the next chapter.

NARROWING DOWN THE SHORTLIST

You now have a longlist of stories. What's the ratio of longlisted stories to stories you need? This tells you how picky you should be.

For example, if you want twenty stories and have a longlist of 200, you know that you'll need to eliminate most. But if you want twenty and your longlist contains only twenty-five, you'll need to include most of them.

At this stage, the main criterion is variety. You want the stories to be as different from each other as possible, while still interpreting the theme, to give the readers a buffet of different flavours.

I move stories from the longlist to the shortlist if they're different in one of the following aspects:

- **Setting.** If almost all the submissions are set in the USA, then the stories set in Botswana, Thailand and Greece make it to the shortlist

- **Point-of-View.** For an anthology of wedding stories, most submissions may be from the bride's, groom's or parent's perspective. The stories with the PoV of the priest, photographer, caterer, wedding organiser, cleaner, flower-girl or ex-wife stand out

- **Tone.** I like to mix funny stories with serious ones, and humour is often in short supply. So any story which makes me chuckle goes on the shortlist. (Of course, this applies only if the tone is appropriate for the theme)

- **Cross-genre.** Stories which straddle genres (the anthology's genre plus one other) add variety and are welcome. For example, if you edit a Horror anthology, then a Western/ Horror story adds a welcome fresh flavour

- **Grabbing power.** Any piece which grabbed you, for whatever reason, deserves a place on the shortlist

Now you should be left with a shortlist of slightly more stories than you will need.

Decline promptly the ones you've eliminated – don't keep the writers waiting for your decision.

I suggest that you notify the shortlisted writers with an update, for example, "Your story is on the shortlist for this anthology. We expect to make the final decision within four weeks."

MAKING THE FINAL CHOICE

At this stage, your mind will be whirring: so many tales, all about the same theme, many of them similar. When I reach this point, I find it a struggle to evaluate the individual stories' merits.

I suggest you get a fresh pair of eyes – or several – by inviting fans of the genre to give their opinions. Ask them one simple question: "Which of these stories are your five favourites?" Their reactions are invaluable, because they are the kind of readers who normally buy this kind of book. Any story they name among their top favourites is worth including.

The other criterion for the final line-up: how much work does this story need? Although all submissions should already be revised and edited to a high standard, there'll be flaws you need to correct. One writer's dialogue punctuation is all wrong, another's sentences tend to run on and need de-convoluting, while a third has overused 'started to' or some other words.

Often, there's an aspect of the plot or structure that needs improving. For example, if the middle drags or a section of the dialogue doesn't sound realistic, you can ask the authors to change it. You'll need to explain why this will improve the story, and ask if they agree and are willing to carry out the change request. Tell them that you will decide about the acceptance once you receive the revised version. You'll then need to work with them, perhaps reading multiple versions and chasing up overdue submissions, until they get it right.

Editing an anthology takes a lot of time, and you can save yourself work by preferring manuscripts which are already close to perfection.

Once you have made your final decision, offer those writers a contract. Don't send the contract yet. Remind them what the terms are, and ask them if the story is still available. You may want to tell the authors what made their story stand out. "I love the sensitive way you've approached this difficult topic." "The members of the editing team are impressed by your understanding of the subject and the skilful way you built suspense." "Your story stood out because of the quirky humour." Getting praise from an editor who accepted a story is one of the most joyful moments in a writer's life.

Delay rejecting the other shortlisted stories until the final line-up is confirmed. Sometimes, writers withdraw stories, perhaps because they don't want to carry out the revisions, or because the pieces have already been accepted elsewhere. Then it's good to have a reserve of shortlisted stories you can draw from.

STRATEGY FOR SUCCESS

If you announce an open-call anthology, you may receive more submissions than you can handle, and most of them will likely not be good enough for serious consideration.

Enlist helpers – perhaps volunteers from your writers' group, perhaps a paid virtual assistant – to wade through the deluge, discard all obviously unsuitable entries and present you with a longlist. Give them clear criteria: form, genre and theme. This way, you need to deal only with submissions which are worth your attention.

FROM MY PERSONAL EXPERIENCE

I'm high-profile in the social media, and this draws trolls and quarrellers. Sometimes, people attack me because I don't share their political views. Among other things, I've been called a 'white male misogynist' (they didn't even bother to check my gender) and a 'Nazi' (on no other grounds than that I'm German).

I simply take note of the trolls' names and identities. Astonishingly often, these people submit stories to my anthologies a year or two later. They've forgotten the unpleasant exchange; I haven't.

Like most editors, I keep a list of writers not to consider. Anyone on that list will have their story rejected unread.

Surprisingly many writers submit stories which are utterly unsuitable. Whenever they see a call for submission, they send their stories, without studying the Guidelines for Contributors. Sometimes, I've pointed out to these writers that they missed the theme. But frankly, anyone who doesn't take the time to read what we want doesn't deserve our time for a reply.

When I prepared to publish the anthology *Cutlass: Ten Tales of Pirates,* a writer sent a High Fantasy story about a battle of orcs. Pirates weren't even mentioned. Since I knew her from social media, I wanted to be courteous and pointed out that the story didn't fit the theme. The author then used her writing app's 'replace' function to change every instance of the word 'orc' into 'pirate' and resubmitted. She didn't even know what pirates were, and thought it didn't matter. Naturally, I declined.

ASSIGNMENTS

1. Create your own list of criteria by which you will choose stories. Although yours should be similar to mine, your project may have some additional or different requirements.

2. Sort the criteria into three groups: from dross to longlist, from longlist to shortlist, and from shortlist to final selection.

CHAPTER 11

SAMPLE LETTERS OF REJECTION AND ACCEPTANCE

Here are some sample letters for correspondence with submitting authors, letting them know whether you will or won't include their story. Feel free to model your own letters on these, changing details to fit the situation and to suit your personal voice.

These days, most of these letters are sent by email.

SAMPLE FIRST-ROUND REJECTION LETTER

Keep rejection letters for unsuitable stories impersonal but courteous. Include just enough information to show which story it is you're rejecting. Don't discourage unskilled writers, because they may improve. Don't provide reasons for your rejection, because this can trigger volatile egos and make you the target of their outrage.

Dear Writer,

Thank you for submitting your story 'A Tale of Two Turtles' for consideration. Unfortunately, it has not been selected because it's not quite what the editors want for this project.

We wish you well in placing your story elsewhere.

Yours sincerely

Editorial Team

SAMPLE REJECTION FOR SHORTLISTED STORIES

Although rejections are disappointing, many writers find it heartening to know that their story was among those shortlisted for serious consideration. Without going into details about the reasons for the rejection, write in a warm and personal tone. These authors are worth cultivating, because their next submission may be exactly right.

Dear Suzie Scrybe,

Thank you for offering 'A Tale of Two Turtles' for publication. Although I liked your story a lot and included it in the shortlist, I'm afraid it didn't make the final cut. I hope it will find a good home soon.

I'd be happy to consider your work for future anthologies, and hope you will submit again.

Yours sincerely

Eddie Torr
Anthology Editor

SAMPLE SHORTLIST LETTER

If a story is in the running, but you need more time to decide, it's helpful to let the author know. Writers are pleased when their story makes it to the shortlist, and they appreciate knowing where they stand. Keep the letter short, so as not to raise unrealistic hopes, and don't open discussions at this stage.

Dear Suzie Scrybe,

Thank you for submitting to Wedding Vows and Bows.

Your submission 'A Tale of Two Turtles' is on our shortlist for serious consideration. We expect to make the final decision by 18 November.

Should the story get accepted elsewhere in the meantime, please let us know.

Yours sincerely

Eddie Torr
Anthology Editor

SAMPLE ACCEPTANCE LETTER

With this acceptance letter, you're initiating a working relationship, so make it both personal and businesslike.

Dear Suzie Scrybe,

It is my pleasure to tell you that your story 'A Tale of Two Turtles' has been selected for the anthology Wedding Vows and Bows. *Your story stood out because of the vivid experience of a traditional Jewish wedding, and everyone on the editorial team loved your witty dialogue.*

Is the story still available? If yes, are you willing to make small changes? Several paragraphs would benefit from tightening to improve the pacing, and I have a suggestion how to rephrase the ending for greater impact.

Subject to these changes, I want to offer you a contract. As per the Guidelines for Contributors, we buy First Rights, exclusive for one year. For this, we pay a flat fee of $150 on publication.

Please let me know if you want to proceed. I look forward to working with you.

Yours sincerely

Eddie Torr
Anthology Editor

NOVICE MISTAKE TO AVOID

Don't enter into discussions about why you reject a story. Many first-time editors mean to be helpful and explain why a story isn't right. Unfortunately, many writers have big egos and respond with vitriolic replies. "You're too stupid to recognise great literature when you get the chance." "You accepted Suzie Scrybe's story, and I'm a much better writer than her." "If my story doesn't suit the theme, then you should change the theme to suit the story!" "I've replaced the word 'birthday' with 'wedding', and I expect you to publish the story now."

A rejecting editor's advice seldom meets with gratitude, but often hostility. Save yourself the stress. It's not your job to teach these people how to write.

There's only one exception: if you personally invited an author to submit to a closed anthology, then you owe them an explanation why you don't want their story after all.

STRATEGY FOR SUCCESS

Inform authors promptly about your decision. Don't keep them hanging in suspense, uncertain of the status. Your fast response will be appreciated and build a positive reputation.

MISTAKES I MADE AND LEARNT FROM

Like almost every new anthology editor, I wanted to be helpful and provide reasons for my rejection. I was sure that the writers would be grateful for these hints.

Alas, instead of gratitude I received accusations and aggression. Writers complained, "You obviously haven't read the story properly" and "You don't know great literature when you see it."

Several wrote back, "Since you don't understand the story, let me explain it to you…"

Others responded by fixing the flaws I had pointed out. "I've changed the ending for you. Now I insist that you publish the story."

Some used swearwords and hurled insults (everything from 'you f…ing imbecile' to 'bl…y Nazi' and 'concussed donkey'), harangued me on social media, slandered me in writers' forums, reported my 'incompetence' to authors' societies to which I belonged, and posted scathing reviews on bookselling sites.

In my inexperience, I responded to their rants, trying to reason. This only incensed them further.

I've learnt from my mistake. Now I stick to standard rejection letters for unsuitable stories, and if anyone hounds me, I hit 'block'. I also add the troublemakers to my list of writers to avoid, and reject their future offerings unread.

ASSIGNMENT

Search your soul. Do you see yourself as a benevolent editor who patiently gives advice to writers whose stories aren't up to the mark?

If yes, spend a few minutes imagining what it's like to receive a barrage of hate mail and to get hounded on social media. Is this really what you want?

Steel yourself, and do not provide explanations to the authors of unsuitable stories. They will learn or give up, and either is a good outcome. You don't need to sacrifice your precious time and nerves.

Compose a standard rejection. Keep it courteous, but free from justifications and value judgements.

CHAPTER 12

WHAT KIND OF DIVERSITY DO YOU WANT?

As the anthology's editor, it's your responsibility not only to create diversity, but to decide what kind of diversity you seek.

'Diversity' can mean many things, most of which are desirable – but not all kinds of diversity are right for every anthology. It's usually best to set a goal of a specific kind of diversity, and restrict the project in other aspects.

There's diversity of form, of content, of authorship – and each of these has many subcategories. Let's look at some of them.

DIVERSITY OF FORM

You mix short stories of varying lengths, articles, anecdotes, poems, letters and so on. This is not usually a good idea, because it would be difficult to sell – unless the anthology is otherwise very restricted, e.g. an anthology about lesbian weddings, with only lesbian authors contributing.

DIVERSITY OF CONTENT

Think this through carefully. On the one hand, you want a tight focus, which will help with market-positioning and sales. On the other hand, you want to treat your readers to variety.

My advice is to focus on the theme – whether that's 'Weddings', 'British Seaside', 'Mother's Day' or 'Rescuing Cats' – and aim for variety in most other content matters.

You can restrict the setting, e.g. only stories set in Arkansas, or only stories set in mountains somewhere in the world. Or you can allow any setting, but specify the main character, e.g. the tales need to be about mature women or about handsome firefighters. The genre can also be varied or limited, e.g. Whodunits or stories of Paranormal Romance.

DIVERSITY OF AUTHORSHIP

In the 20th century, many anthology editors accepted mostly stories by white male authors, some deliberately, others because of a subconscious bias. Today's anthology editors often seek to create more balance in their anthologies by including tales from writers of different backgrounds.

Some editors even seek to address the issue by including only submissions by previously under-represented writers, for example, by publishing only stories by women or by ethnic minorities. Of course, those books don't have diversity of authorship, but they help balance out previous inequalities.

If you aim for diversity of authorship, you face the problem of how to know which author ticks which box. How do you know if a submitting author is truly disabled, transgendered, of Maltese nationality or Cherokee descent? What if writers claim to belong to a certain ethnic minority or pretend a sexual orientation, just to improve their chances of acceptance? How are you going to verify their claims? Not every aspect can be asserted with a simple passport scan, and you could spend more time investigating the authors' backgrounds than editing the anthology.

If you specifically want stories from writers of certain backgrounds, the phrase 'identify as' is a solution. For example, 'We publish stories from authors who identify as gay' (or as Asian, Black, Pagan, asexual, mentally disabled…). You can even include a sentence in the contract in which the writer confirms this self-identification.

MY CHOICES FOR MY ANTHOLOGIES

I don't select or discard submissions for the sake of balanced authorship statistics. Frankly, I don't think the writer's gender or skin colour matters. What counts is the story.

However, I actively strive for cultural diversity. By this I mean stories set in different geographical locations and in different social contexts, with different beliefs and traditions. I want authors who understand these cultural contexts so well – perhaps because they live there, or came from those origins – that they can write about them with insight and authenticity.

I also seek diversity of settings, so I can take the readers on a virtual journey to many different places.

These are the criteria I have decided on for my anthologies. You may choose different criteria for yours.

PROFESSIONAL TIP

When deciding on the criteria for diversity and inclusiveness, keep in mind the reason why you're producing this anthology.

Do you want to create awareness for the plight of a social group, improve representation for an ethnic minority, showcase your local writers' group, inspire people of your faith to lead chaste lives, or give readers a book crammed with action-packed suspense?

Whatever your purpose, it will define how inclusive or exclusive you need to be in at least one aspect. Stick with this.

WHAT NOT TO DO

Don't let haters and slanderers get to you. Whatever you decide, these days it's likely that someone will take offence. Often, these are trolls who scour the internet for something to take offence at.

Sometimes they're writers who weren't invited to submit, or whose stories you declined.

If you limit submissions by authorship (e.g. you accept submissions only from people of a specific ethnicity or gender orientation), it's likely that some of those who don't fall into that group will complain and voice their anger in the social media. "This editor is racist because she accepts submissions only from Black people." "The editor rejected my story. He claimed the story was not what he was looking for, but I know it's because I'm Black. Unfair!" "This women-only anthology is sexist. Men, stand up for your rights and boycott this book!"

Even if you have great diversity in your authorship, there'll be hecklers. "Brunettes are under-represented in this book! 61% of Paranormal Steampunk Romance writers are brunettes, but this book has only one single brunette-authored story."

Don't engage with trolls and disgruntled writers. Simply ignore them. They'll soon find something or someone else to rant about.

If a complainer seems genuinely upset and communicates with politeness, respond courteously. Thank them for bringing the matter to your attention. Express your regret that this particular project isn't completely inclusive, and add a one-sentence explanation why this was not possible. Say that you will consider their comments when planning future projects. Then disengage.

MISTAKES I MADE AND LEARNT FROM

When I first encouraged authors from other countries and cultures, I was disappointed that they all sent stories set in the USA instead of their home countries. I learnt to request specifically stories with a flavour of their country, showing lush settings, traditions, rituals and attitudes.

ASSIGNMENT

Decide in which areas you will keep your anthology tightly focused, in which you will actively seek diversity, and in which you'll just allow the selection to develop organically.

There is no single 'right' answer: you need to find what is best for this individual project.

CHAPTER 13

PUBLISHING WRITERS' GROUP SHOWCASE ANTHOLOGY

Writers' groups are often keen to publish anthologies, showcasing the members' works. For many writers this is the first-ever experience of getting published, an exciting achievement. When you volunteer to be the editor (or get volunteered, perhaps because you're the group's leader, or the most experienced writer of the group) you'll take on specific challenges.

EXPECTATIONS

Lacking experience in the publishing field, many new writers have unrealistic expectations, believing that publication will lead to instant fame, and that literary agents will knock on their door and publishers will start a bidding war. You may need to bring them – gently – down to earth.

GENRE, THEME AND FORMAT

The type of group determines the contents. Local writers' groups often cover a broad range of writing (fiction, journalism, blogs, memoirs, poetry) as well as genres (Romance, Thriller, Horror, Fantasy…) and this can make it difficult to stick to just one form and genre.

What members of local writers' groups have in common is their location. Turn this into an advantage by choosing the locality as a theme, e.g. stories and poems about Chicago, about the Scottish Lowlands, about the Cornish coast.

Choosing a local theme brings a huge marketing advantage. Whereas most writers' groups' anthologies scarcely sell to anyone other than group members and their families, an anthology with a local theme often gets snapped up by local shops.

Organise a series of workshops to help members craft tales about the theme. An experienced member may volunteer to lead those sessions, or you may bring in an outside instructor. This will speed up the writing process and ensure that you get quality submissions.

RAISING THE STANDARDS

In most writers' groups, members are learners of varying skill levels. This means that some of the stories won't be of a high standard.

Since the purpose is to showcase members' works, there's the expectation that everyone will be included, and you can't simply reject the substandard submissions.

The solution is to coax and coach the members and help them improve their stories. If possible, involve the more advanced members and ask them to mentor the novices during the project. Each mentor helps one novice to craft and improve their submission and to maintain their schedule.

Explain to the group that you want this anthology to be 'professional', that you want it to look professional, and filled with professional-quality writing, not a feeble amateur effort like most local writers' groups' publications, but a book to be proud of. Tell them that you believe they have it in them, but that they'll have to work, learn and revise a lot to achieve this standard. "Are you willing to do this?"

In my experience, the word 'professional' has a galvanising effect. Local writers' groups love the idea that they can produce a professional level anthology, and the prospect of outdoing other writers' groups fires their enthusiasm. I've always received a resounding 'yes, let's create a professional book' from all members, from novice to seasoned author.

Of course, genuine 'professional' level may not be attainable, but you can strive towards it. The resulting book will be several notches above typical local writers' group anthologies.

DEALING WITH AMATEURS

If members of your group are new writers, you may need to lower your expectations, not only regarding the quality of their work, but about their professionalism. Keep in mind that you are dealing with a bunch of amateurs who will have little understanding of the publishing business. It will be up to you to mediate between their delusions and the realities of the marketplace.

You may need to deal with their egos – some of them inflated, others fragile – by applying tact and diplomacy, gentle support and firm instructions. Give motivating talks, praise their skills and progress, share your enthusiasm for the project.

Many planned writers' group anthology projects fizzle out. Members begin filled with enthusiasm and promises, and then don't follow through. Some lose interest in the book or their story, others drop out of the group to pursue different hobbies. When working with a group of amateurs, you need to provide the motivation, structure and staying power for all of them.

If you manage the project well, members will benefit hugely. Their writing skills will rise to a higher level, they'll learn the basics of how to submit to publishers, and they'll acquire professional attitudes.

EXPERIENCED MEMBERS

If your group includes members of different skill levels, involve the experienced writers in the editing process. This will take some of the workload off you and give them useful insights. They can also coach and mentor novices to bring their stories up to scratch.

Seasoned authors welcome the additional publication credit, but are understandably reluctant to give their unpublished works with the precious 'first rights' to an amateur anthology. Allow them to contribute previously published stories instead, provided those fit the theme.

SCHEDULE

The biggest challenge in working with a bunch of newbies is how to get them to adhere to a schedule. They may not understand the meaning and necessity of closing dates.

I recommend that you set two dates: one for submission of the story, the second for carrying out the revisions. Impress on members that these dates are firm and that no extensions will be granted. "We are producing a professional anthology, and it's important that you are professional about this. If you miss one of those dates, your story will not get accepted. Then you will not be represented in this anthology."

GUIDELINES FOR CONTRIBUTORS

Structure the guidelines like you would for any other anthology, but when you use jargon which the writers may not understand, add the 'translation' in parentheses.

Don't demand fancy formatting with specific fonts and indentations, but insist on getting electronic submissions. Otherwise people will give you stories handwritten on lined pink paper, adding to your workload. If some members aren't computer literate, ask for volunteers to do the typing.

Emphasise the closing date for the submission and the date when the revisions must be handed in, and put this paragraph in bold.

TITLE AND SUBTITLE

Choose a catchy title, and add a subtitle which includes either the group's name or a clue about the location, e.g. *Snakebite: Texas Stories by Texas Writers. Spindrift: Stories from the Sussex Seaside.*

ILLUSTRATIONS

Pictures add visual interest to a book. This works especially well for local anthologies with a local theme. Line drawings are best. Perhaps a group member is a skilled artist, or maybe there's a local art group keen to collaborate on a joint project.

When I edited anthologies for a writers' group in England, a student from the local art college was thrilled at the opportunity to get experience and see her work published in a book. She did a great job. We invited her to the book launch where she was celebrated as a star.

PRINTING AND PUBLISHING

Sales will be mostly to local people – residents and visitors who want printed books. Instead of PoD (print on demand, where each copy gets printed and paid individually), I suggest ordering a 'print run', that is a specific number of copies printed at once. Patronise a local printing company, because this will generate local goodwill and make the logistics easier.

The larger the print run, the cheaper each individual copy will be, so get the largest print run that's practical and affordable. However, don't overestimate the number of sales you'll make. You'll probably need one copy for each member (free, not paid-for), and a few more to give away to supporters. Think realistically about how many copies you will be able to sell. Twenty? 200? If the book has a strong local theme and you have a good marketing strategy, you may be able to sell several hundred copies. It's almost unheard of for a local writers' group's anthology to sell more than 1,000.

GRANTS

You may be able to get grants to pay for a workshop leader, illustrations, editing or printing.

Sponsors include the municipality (town council), the regional arts board, philanthropic organisations, lotteries and charities. Some have ongoing programmes, others accept applications once a year. They have clear guidelines about what kind of project they seek to support, what they want to achieve and how groups can apply.

During the years I led groups in Britain, I was able to secure many 'small arts groups' grants for anthologies and other projects, mostly from the British National Lottery, from the regional arts boards and from the local town councils.

Every year, different organisations sponsor different projects with different criteria, so you need to research what is available. Some seek to sponsor specific kinds of people – e.g. over-60s, under-20s, ethnic minorities, Christians, single parents, people with disabilities, the unemployed. If a large portion of your group falls into this category, emphasise this, and your chances are good.

Most organisations are less interested in the product (the book) than in the long-term benefits gained by the members. Focus your application on the skills that participants will learn, such as project management, schedule-planning, time-keeping, budgeting, leadership, team-working, salesmanship. For most grant applications, a list of the skills people will learn which will make them more employable is a veritable 'open sesame' code.

Important: you need to apply for grants before you start producing the book, not after it has been published. This means you have to plan several months – often more than a year – in advance.

MARKETING

An anthology published by a local writers' group sells through local shops.

If your book has a local theme, you'll find that many local shops are keen to stock the book: not just bookstores, but grocers, souvenir shops, art galleries, museums, tourist attractions, bars and coffee shops.

The typical arrangement is 'sale or return' – that is, you leave several copies in the shop, and after some months, the shop will give back the unsold copies and pay you for the sold ones. They keep a commission, which is usually 30% of the retail price.

Whenever there's a local festival, your group can take a stall and sell books. Consider sharing a stall (the fee and the staffing) with someone else, perhaps a self-publishing author or a local artist.

If the book is of high quality, the libraries of the region often also choose to stock it.

When my writers' group in England published anthologies, the town's museums were eager to stock the book, especially our anthology of Sussex seaside stories. The museums' visitors were mostly tourists who wanted a cultured local souvenir, and entertaining short stories in an affordable little book were just right. In one museum, they actually asked our group if we would consider publishing an anthology with the theme 'Smugglers and Pirates' next, because visitors often requested a story book on that theme. (I would have liked to do that, but not all members were interested.)

HOLD A LAUNCH PARTY

Celebrate the new book with a special event to which you invite the public. You can hold the party in a coffee shop, pub or bar (and everyone pays for their own drinks), or you can hire a venue and provide the refreshments. Local art galleries are often keen to host a book launch which entices visitors to their rooms. They provide the venue and chairs, while you bring the refreshments.

Encourage group members to dress smartly and to bring their family and friends. Members read excerpts from their stories (I recommend the opening paragraphs) and pose for photos with the book.

This launch party is a highlight for the group and also a proud moment for the members, many of whom are celebrating their first ever publication. The event is also a media opportunity. Take photos and videos, share them on social media, publish them on the group's website and send them to the local newspaper.

NOVICE MISTAKE TO AVOID

Don't publish an unfocused mishmash of forms, genres and themes. Members may want to offload whatever they have written and expect it to be showcased in the anthology. Be firm and guide them to think like professional writers and publishers.

Don't extend the submission dates to anyone. Otherwise, others will delay submitting as well, over and over, and the book will never get completed.

STRATEGY FOR SUCCESS

Treat the project as a training opportunity for yourself. You'll gain insights into the work of an editor and publisher, and learn team leadership and project management skills. These will stand you in good stead for your future career or publishing business ventures.

FROM MY PERSONAL EXPERIENCE

I've project-managed the publication of anthologies for several writers' groups. The toughest difficulty was always the same: how to get members to keep to the agreed schedule. There's always someone who misses the deadlines, offers up one excuse after another, and expects that everything will be held up for them.

A group member – let's call him Dave – was a novice writer who possessed considerable natural talent, but had not mastered the craft of story writing yet. He produced two stories which showed promise but needed substantial improvement. My co-editor Joe spent hours coaching Dave, and Dave promised to carry out the changes within a month. When the deadline for submitting the revised versions came, Dave said, "I don't have the time. If you want changes, you make them. You have my permission to edit the stories as you see fit."

Joe and I then spent yet more hours rewriting Dave's stories, and sent them to him for approval. Dave didn't respond, despite reminders.

Joe and I put the anthology together and formatted it. The day before it was due at the printer's, Dave finally got in touch: "I don't like the changes you made. I withdraw my stories."

What now? Joe and I scrambled to salvage the project so as not to lose our booked slot at the printer's and the funding we'd received from the arts board. We were both seasoned short story writers, and we each sacrificed the precious first rights of an unpublished story which would otherwise have earned us good money. We worked all night to rewrite our own stories to give them a local setting.

The next day, I cancelled all my commitments and redid the book's formatting. Exhausted from stress and lack of sleep, Joe and I managed to rush the book to the printer's, with just twenty minutes to spare.

Then the group members bickered because Joe and I each had three stories in the anthology, while the others had only one or two. They complained that we had abused our position to push our own works at the expense of other members.

Sadly, this kind of situation is common when you deal with inexperienced writers whose egos are bigger than their professionalism.

On a positive note, I want to tell you about an interesting marketing experience.

One year, we had a surprising marketing success. One of the group's sales team went into a delicatessen to offer the book. The managers exclaimed, "This is just what we need!" They were selling Sussex-themed gift hampers for Christmas: Sussex cheese, Sussex wine, Sussex sausage and other locally-produced edibles. They wanted something a bit different, inexpensive yet classy, of course Sussex-themed. An anthology of Sussex ghost stories, written by Sussex authors, was exactly right. They ordered more books than any other shop, and even placed a reorder for yet more.

ASSIGNMENT

Choose the theme for your group's anthology, keeping in mind the members' interests and marketing benefits.

CHAPTER 14

PUBLISHING A FUNDRAISING ANTHOLOGY

Do you want to publish a book to raise funds for a good cause? This can be a collection of your own stories, or an anthology of multiple authors' works. In this chapter, I've compiled the practical pointers you need.

WHO ARE THE FUNDS FOR?

Do you want to boost the finances for your backpacking trip, raise funds for your local cat shelter, or support a major charity?

Are you going to give all the income from the book to the cause, or only the profit (after deducting expenses)? You need to be clear in your mind and upfront with your readers.

If the funds are intended for a registered charity, that organisation needs to confirm the arrangement, to prevent fraud.

SELECTING THE THEME

Choose a theme which reflects the purpose. Are you raising funds for your local cat rescue shelter or for a soup kitchen? Then create a book with stories about cats or about food. This will appeal to the kind of people who care about the cause, and get your book talked about in the right circles.

However, don't restrict the theme too tightly. Otherwise you may find it difficult to get enough quality submissions. A call for stories about cats will bring in many entries from which you can choose the best. But if you ask for tales about motherless kittens rescued during a snowstorm in the mountains, the yield may be too sparse to produce an anthology.

FICTION OR NON-FICTION?

You can have fiction or non-fiction. But I advise against mixing the two.

For a **fiction** book, opt for short stories, perhaps supplemented with poems. You may want to be flexible about the genre. The contributions need to show the purpose in a positive light. Taking the example of an anthology in support of a cat rescue shelter, the cats should be gentle, resourceful, brave and kind – not vicious and evil. Prefer an upbeat tone: harrowing things may happen, but the outcome should be positive and ideally heart-warming.

For a **non-fiction** anthology, invite people to share their experiences. Let's say you want to create a fundraiser-book for a charity supporting the homeless. Then you ask homeless – and formerly homeless – people to write about their life on the streets, how they got into that situation, how they got out of it, the ordeals they survived, the unexpected moments of kindness they found. Select contributions which are vivid and convey a message of hope. Hardships should be described in a realistic but not overly graphic way. To avoid legal troubles (such as libel claims), leave out or change the names of bad people. Depending on the nature of the subject, some authors may not want to be identified, for example because recognition would endanger their safety. Respect this request and allow contributors to use a pseudonym if they wish.

FINDING STORIES

You can fill the collection with your own tales (in which case it's not an anthology, but a simple collection, and probably won't sell well unless you have an established fan base) or invite submissions from other writers.

In addition to the usual avenues (described in the relevant chapter), the charity's supporters are a good source, because they care about the cause. Aim for an announcement in the organisation's newsletter and social media.

Also ask established authors for stories. Many will be happy to let you use previously published pieces, free of charge.

HOW MUCH YOU CAN EXPECT TO RAISE

Let me tell you upfront, you probably won't raise as much money as you envisage. Publishing a book is rarely a very profitable venture. I've known editors who invested almost 100 hours in a project and raised less than US$10. With a well-chosen theme and a solid marketing strategy, you can of course achieve substantially more. Some anthologies reach up to around US$1,000, but that's rare.

Be aware that the work that goes into publishing an anthology is not likely to pay off in a big way. It's usually a trickle of income rather than a flood.

Consider the non-financial benefits, too, both for the charity and yourself. The project may provide not just money but welcome positive publicity for the cause, and you can have a lot of fun and learn useful skills.

PAYING THE AUTHORS

Some fundraising anthologies pay a token fee, others don't. Another possibility is to offer a fee, and give the selected writers the option to donate it to the cause. This is a popular choice because it makes writers feel good for getting paid and for helping.

ACCOUNTING

If you raise funds for a charitable organisation, you will need to keep meticulous accounts to prevent accusations and slander. Be prepared to provide detailed statements of your income and expenses. This bookkeeping work can take up a lot of time.

I recommend that you keep the fundraising anthology separate from your other publishing ventures, otherwise the income and expenditure can be difficult to detangle.

NOVICE MISTAKE TO AVOID

If you haven't been able to find buyers and readers for your own stories, don't publish a fundraising book in the expectation that your writing will reach an audience this way. You'll be disappointed.

STRATEGY FOR SUCCESS

Get a well-known person to write a foreword – the director of the charity, a subject expert, a local celebrity. This validates the book in the eyes of potential buyers and will help greatly with the marketing.

Let's say you want to raise funds for a local cat rescue shelter. You could ask the shelter's director, the town's veterinarian, or the movie actress who lives locally and is known to love cats.

FROM MY PERSONAL EXPERIENCE

Many times, writers have approached me and asked me to contribute a story to their planned fundraising anthology. While I'm happy to help first-time anthology editors, especially if it's for a good cause, I always ask them a few questions about their vision for the project before I decide.

Surprisingly many don't have a clear vision, let alone a sound marketing strategy. All they have is a vague idea to put all kinds of stories into a book, which will bring in lots of money somehow. This clueless, haphazard approach won't result in a quality book, let alone raise funds. To be included in such a book would be embarrassing, so I say no.

If the project sounds realistic – for example, it has a theme and a basic marketing plan– and if I have a suitable previously published story, I'm happy to let the publisher include it.

ASSIGNMENT

What theme best encapsulates the spirit of the cause? Who are the potential buyers for this book? How and where will you sell the book?

CHAPTER 15

THE PUBLISHING AGREEMENT

To prevent problems arising later, draw up a contract for each writer. Both parties (you as the publisher, and they, as the contributors) need to agree to it formally.

REASONS FOR THE CONTRACT

Simply put, confirming the agreement in writing saves problems.

- Laying the terms out clearly ends misunderstandings. Perhaps a writer has previously misheard what you said, or confused your anthology with a different project. This is their final chance to withdraw

- A contract clarifies who has committed to what, e.g. that the writer permits you to publish the story, and you promise to pay for it

- It makes new writers feel good. For novices who've never been published before, the first publishing contract is a thrilling moment

- It indemnifies you against certain problems – e.g. if a writer has committed libel or plagiarism, you won't get the blame

- Years later, when verbal assurances and casual communications have become a hazy memory, the written contract reminds everyone what was agreed

- In case of a legal dispute, it shows what the parties agreed to

Please note: I'm not a lawyer, and my suggestions in this chapter don't constitute legal advice. If your project involves large sums of money or potentially libellous content, or if you have reason to believe that one of the authors hasn't been honest, consult a lawyer.

My recommendation is to avoid legal problems. If a writer is quarrelsome or if the authorship of a story is in dispute, drop them rather than take any risks. Even the most brilliant story isn't worth a legal battle.

In my experience, putting everything in writing is the best way to avoid later problems. Writers don't want to get drawn into legal disputes any more than you do, so spend the time and draw up a simple contract.

WHAT TO PUT INTO THE AGREEMENT

- The author's name and the title of the story

- The publisher's name and the title (or working title) of the anthology

- What rights does the author assign to you? This is the most important part of the agreement. Reread the chapter about rights, to make sure you understand this issue. In the case of First Rights, I recommend a 'rights reversal' clause to protect the authors

- What will the author receive from you? For example, how much will you pay when?

- The author affirms that the story is their creation, and that they own all rights

- A sentence stating that the author will be identified as the creator of this story

- How much editing are you allowed to do?

- The author indemnifies the publisher against any legal claims arising from the story, e.g. libel and plagiarism

- Any additional commitments

- The date and signature or, in case of emailed agreements, 'I agree' and name

FORMAT OF THE AGREEMENT

You can simply send the agreement in the body of an email, and the writer adds 'I agree with this. Date, Name.' This is sufficient for most purposes.

A more formal version (but technically not feasible for everyone) is to print the contract, sign it by hand, scan it, then send it as an attachment, which the writer prints out, signs, scans and sends back.

If you live locally, exchanging paper contracts is straightforward and preferable.

WHEN TO SEND THE CONTRACT

The time to send the contract is when the writer has completed the final edits and the story is ready for publication. I advise against contracts before the story is ready.

WHAT IF A WRITER DOESN'T WANT TO SIGN?

If a writer delays committing to the agreement or balks at a certain clause, that's a red flag.

Perhaps he no longer owns the rights to this story because he sold 'all rights' to another publisher. Maybe he tried to pass off someone else's story as his work, and now he's getting cold feet.

Sometimes, a writer didn't read the Guidelines for Contributors before submitting, and realises belatedly that she doesn't like the terms. She may have missed the fact that this was a 'for the luv' project, and assumed that she was going to get paid a lot of money.

Instead of arguing, simply withdraw your offer for publication and select another piece from the shortlist. While it's frustrating to lose a good story, it's also a reason to rejoice: you've dodged a bullet.

SAMPLE PUBLISHING AGREEMENT

Publishing Agreement

Suzie Scrybe gives Eddie Torr the permanent non-exclusive right to publish the story 'Six Sprigs of Heather' in an anthology of love stories with the working title Highland Proposals: Scottish Tales of Romance.

This book may be published in different formats, e.g. ebook, paperback, audiobook.

Suzie Scrybe retains all rights to the story and may publish it elsewhere. Eddie Torr does not have the right to publish the story other than in this anthology.

In the book, Suzie Scrybe will be identified as the author and copyright holder of the story.

Eddie Torr may edit the story as he deems necessary for grammar, spelling, punctuation and minor style matters. He does not have the right to make any changes to the content.

Suzie Scrybe asserts that she is the creator of this story and owns all rights. She indemnifies Eddie Torr against any legal claims arising from this story.

On publication, Eddie Torr will pay Suzie Scrybe GBP 20 for the use of the story. Payment will be made by PayPal or direct bank transfer.

Suzie Scrybe gives Eddie Torr the right to use the book cover for personal and promotional purposes.

When the book is published, Suzie Scrybe will receive a complete formatted ebook as well as a paperback copy.

NOVICE MISTAKE TO AVOID

Don't rely on verbal agreements and casual conversations on social media. Those can be misunderstood or mislaid. A written agreement is crucial.

STRATEGY FOR SUCCESS

Give all contributors identical contracts. This will simplify your work and prevent resentment among the writers.

FROM MY PERSONAL EXPERIENCE

I find that having a written agreement effectively prevents problems.

Sometimes, authors raised questions about a clause. "What if...?" Each time, I was able to point them to another clause which answered their query. I've published stories by professional authors, and they always found my written agreements to be sensible and to the point.

There were a few occasions when I 'lost' a writer at the contract stage, and while this created stress – needing to replace the story at very short notice – I was glad that I'd dodged a bullet with those writers.

One writer finally confessed, "I don't want to sign this clause because I sold 'all rights' to this story ten years ago, but I'm sure this doesn't matter." Uh-uh. This sort of thing matters a lot, and I withdrew my offer immediately.

A novice writer got so excited by the prospect of her first-ever publication that she hired a lawyer to draw up a different contract – one that ran over twelve pages, covering film rights, abbreviation rights, the pictorial representation of characters and more, appropriate for a novel, but not for a short story in an anthology. The story itself was only four pages long.

I declined, pointing out that this was a standard contract, the same for all contributors. She insisted: "Either you sign my contract, or I won't let you publish my story." Did this wannabe really think she had that kind of negotiation power? The story, while nice, wasn't outstanding, and I had plenty of other submissions to choose from. I thanked her for her interest in my anthology and withdrew my publication offer.

ASSIGNMENT

Create a rough draft for your publishing agreement.

CHAPTER 16

EDITING THE ANTHOLOGY

When you publish a collection of your own stories, the editing process is simple. You revise each story in the same way as you revise your other works, seeking feedback and critiques from other writers and beta readers and choosing which of their suggestions to apply. With an anthology, editing involves a lot more. This chapter is a guide how to work with authors to improve their stories.

CONTENT EDITING

If the content needs improving – perhaps the middle needs tightening because the pacing is slack, or a character needs more development or a different structure would give the ending more impact – don't carry out those changes yourself. You don't have the right to do this, and it's not your job. Explain the improvements you want, and why. It's the author's decision whether to consent to those change requests, and the author's job to carry them out.

Important: state any change requests before you accept the story. Once the agreement is signed, it's too late. Some authors will decline to alter their piece because the proposed changes don't suit their vision for the piece, and others simply can't be bothered to do more work.

Once a story has been accepted, avoid altering the contents. If you discover belatedly that a flaw needs fixing, liaise with the author about it. "At the end of the scene, Amelia takes off her shoes. But she was already barefoot earlier in the scene. I think this needs to be consistent, do you agree? Do you want to tweak this yourself, or do you prefer if I fix it?"

COPY-EDITING

Copy edits are small improvements at sentence level for clarity and flow. For example, if a sentence is long and convoluted, you can break it into two shorter sentences, and if a certain noun is used four times in one paragraph, you can replace it with synonyms.

Watch out especially for words overused by novice writers, such as *look, could, start to, begin to.* These can often be replaced or simply deleted. *(As soon as she could hear the motor howling she started to run* can be copyedited to *As soon as she heard the motor howl, she ran.)* But don't make elaborate changes, even if those would improve the writing. It's not the editor's job to alter the writer's voice.

The contract should allow you to carry out copy-edits without asking.

PROOFREADING

Checking for errors of grammar, spelling, syntax and punctuation comes last, after the whole book manuscript is assembled. It's a good idea to involve a fresh pair of eyes here, because the author who wrote a story and the editor who worked on it will see what they know should be there, and miss errors. Hire a proofreader if your budget allows it.

You can swap services with other editors and writers: you proofread their book, and they read yours. For a showcase anthology, e.g. a writers' group's project, members with good spelling skills can volunteer to read each other's works. Ask them to mark the errors they spotted with margin comments or track changes, not to apply the corrections themselves.

BRITISH AND AMERICAN ENGLISH

If you publish an international anthology, the contributors will use different forms of the English language in their writing. US

American and British (and Australian) English use different spellings, e.g. honour/honor, colour/color, realise/realize, travelling/traveling. The vocabulary varies, too, e.g. autumn/fall, elevator/lift, railway/railroad. Some syntax and punctuation rules differ as well, and some words are used differently. For example, American English writers use 'that' in many cases where correct British English demands 'which'. Neither is wrong or better. They're just different.

For an anthology editor, this creates a conundrum: should the whole book be in British English or in American English, or should you leave every story as it is?

In my anthologies, I keep the American and British versions of the English language as written. This saves me work, and it keeps the authors' voices intact.

If your theme has a local flavour, e.g. Whodunit stories set in Australia, or Western stories set in Arizona, it makes sense to apply the regional version of English to the whole book, even if some of the contributors live elsewhere.

NOVICE MISTAKE TO AVOID

Don't work with stories which need substantial rewriting. It's not your job to act as an unpaid writing coach. You may feel noble and generous, giving a leg-up to new writers – but after you've given them many hours of your precious work, many writers don't deliver the final versions because they 'don't have the time'. Some even take advantage, deliberately use you as a writing coach and editor whom they don't have to pay, and then withdraw the submission and sell the improved version to a better paying market instead.

STRATEGY FOR SUCCESS

If you include both British and American English stories, say so in the foreword. For example: "To preserve the authors' individual voices, I've left the differences between American and British English."

Otherwise, some readers may find the inconsistency confusing, or even think that these are uncorrected spelling errors, and post scathing reviews.

FROM MY EXPERIENCE

For the first few anthologies I edited, I went out of my way to nurture new writers. Since I didn't offer payment, I thought I ought to be generous with my time. Big mistake.

Several times, I'd spent many hours coaching writers, working with them through multiple revisions of their stories, only for them to drop out.

One case was especially hurtful. The writer was a novice who followed me on social media. He seemed like a nice guy, and I wanted to help him succeed. I told him about the forthcoming 'for the luv' anthology, brainstormed ideas for the theme, helped him develop a plot, taught him professional techniques, and worked with him at every stage of the story. I spent more time mentoring him than it would have taken me to write a story myself. He was enthusiastic and appreciative – but when it came to signing the contract, he delayed until the last minute, and then demanded that I pay for the use of the story.

I reminded him of the terms he had agreed to – this was a 'for the luv' project, none of the writers were getting paid. I explained that the book was already edited, proofread and formatted, and that missing the launch date would have devastating consequences. That's when this writer showed his true colours. "I know. And that's why you will pay me. Either you pay up, or else."

Rayne Hall doesn't give in to blackmail, period.

I postponed publication of the book until I had found and edited another story. This caused me yet more work, and the missed launch impacted sales, but I learnt a valuable lesson. I no longer coach authors whose submissions are not of publishable quality.

Another mistake I made early on was to give contracts to writers before receiving the revised versions. I remember one writer who agreed with the suggested changes and promised to carry them out by the specified date. On that day, she told me that she didn't like the change requests and demanded that I publish the story as it was. Since I had run out of time, I included the story as it was, although it was substandard. As a result, book reviewers commented that 'some stories are better than others' and ratings and sales suffered.

I wouldn't do that again. Anyone who lets me down like that just gets crossed off the list.

These days, I keep a file of shortlisted stories – the ones which were good although not my first choice. If an accepted writer messes me about, I email the author of a shortlisted publication-ready submission. "Is your story still available? If yes, I'd like to include it, because one of the selected stories has fallen through." This situation has arisen twice, and in both cases, the 'substitute' authors agreed happily and caused no problems, so the issue was resolved.

ASSIGNMENT

Decide how much time you are willing to give to each story before the contract is signed, and how much after.

There are no right or wrong answers. If you pay professional rates for the use of stories, they should require minimal editing, but beginner efforts in a writers' group's anthology probably need substantial time input from the editor.

Either way, you need to set clear boundaries, because your time is precious.

DECIDING THE ORDER OF THE STORIES

Once you've selected the stories, decide on the order in which you will put them in the book.

Start by deciding on the first, then the final story, then the rest.

THE FIRST STORY

The first story should have a strong beginning which pulls readers in. It's the part people read when they click 'download free sample', and it needs to appeal to as many readers of the target audience as possible. This means it needs to be well-written, and it also needs a strong hook at the beginning.

It shouldn't be better than the rest of the stories, though. If you raise expectations with a superbly crafted story, and readers buy on the strength of the sample and are disappointed by what follows, they'll leave scathing customer reviews, and this will harm the book and your reputation.

It should be typical of the stories that follow, in content and tone. Don't start with a story that's very different from the rest, because it would raise false expectations. For example, if you have only one humorous story, don't use this to open the anthology. Otherwise readers will expect lots of funny stories, and be disappointed.

THE FINAL STORY

The last tale in the book should have emotional impact and leave the reader thinking. Select a meaningful story with a powerful ending. So when readers close the book, it stays in their minds for some time. The final sentence should be memorable.

THE REST OF THE STORIES

Decide which are the strongest tales. These are often reprints by professional authors. Spread them out. For example, if you have five superb stories in a twenty-story anthology, you may want to make them numbers 1, 5, 15 and 20.

If a story is a little weaker than the others, sandwich it between two better ones. Readers who feel disappointed by one tale will quickly read the next without hard feelings, but if they get two or more weak stories in a row, they'll feel frustrated and set the book aside. (Of course, it's your responsibility to ensure that no seriously weak story makes it into the anthology.)

When arranging the selected stories, aim for variety. Don't put two similar stories back to back. For example, if you have three humorous tales and the rest are earnest, place each of the funnies in a different third of the book. If you have mostly stories but also a few poems, sprinkle the poems across the volume. Similarly, alternate short and long stories, first and third person Point-of-View, short and long pieces. For an anthology of stories set in Britain, you could have a story set in London followed by one set in Scotland, then one in Birmingham, one in the Welsh mountains, one in the Lake District, one on the seashore of Cornwall and so on.

NOVICE MISTAKE TO AVOID

Don't split the book into separate parts to group the stories by subject.

For example, you may plan a book of British tales and group them into 'England', 'Scotland' and 'Wales'. But what if you receive plenty of excellent stories about Scotland, and mostly mediocre ones set in Wales? Will you accept second-rate submissions, just to make the three parts equal?

You'll also face the conundrum of whether you should devote a whole section to 'Cornwall' or include it under 'England'. What about the stories set in Northern Ireland? And how about the Republic of Ireland, which doesn't belong to the United Kingdom but is nevertheless part of the British Isles? Not to mention the Channel Islands, the Falklands and Gibraltar... and where will you put the historical stories set in a country that was a British colony at the time? Whatever you decide, some readers will feel incensed.

A mishmash is much easier to create and less likely to offend.

STRATEGY FOR SUCCESS

Start thinking about the order of the stories early on. When you narrow down the shortlist, you can take notes: "This tale would be great to open the anthology." "Whoa, this story has an emotional impact. It could be the final piece in the book."

FROM MY PERSONAL EXPERIENCE

I find that a structure in which every aspect is perfectly distributed is rarely attainable. If I get the settings and lengths nicely mixed up, I may still end up with several stories with similar main characters or similar moods close together. It can feel like a mental puzzle to which no solution exists. I've learnt to aim for a good mix rather than to chase the elusive perfection.

ASSIGNMENT

Study a single-author collection or anthology in your genre. How did the editor choose the first and final stories? Would you have arranged the order differently?

CHAPTER 18

ADD VALUE WITH LITTLE EXTRAS

In this chapter, I'm going to suggest optional 'extras' you can add to hook and satisfy readers.

TEASER LINES

Under each story title, write a sentence to entice the readers to delve into the tale.

Here are the story titles and teaser lines from my anthology *The Haunted Train: Creepy Tales from the Railways.*

Frederick Langridge: Beware of Tuesdays
Will the railway ghost still show herself?

Clint Spivey: The Drowned Subway
A commuter in Tokyo travels on a subway train filled with unusual passengers.

JD Beresford: Lost in the Fog
After taking the wrong train, I must spend a cold foggy night in remote railway station.

Nicole Tait: Why are Trains Always Late?
A late-night trip, a woman alone.

Edith Wharton: The Journey
Will this journey take her to the freedom she craves?

Morgan A. Pryce: 11th Hour Ghost Train to Siam
When midnight approaches, a special kind of Bangkokians ride the Skytrain.

Rayne Hall: Funicular Fare
In Edwardian England, a werewolf takes the funicular railway.

Andrew M Seddon: Wolf Station
A train engineer makes an unscheduled stop in the Carpathian Mountains.

Petina Strohmer: Gallows Curve
A notorious accident blackspot has one last life to claim.

Amelia Edwards: The 4.15 Express
Was it really John Dwerrihouse who travelled with me on that train?

Pia Manning: Bon Appétit
A pledge candidate will do anything to join an elite fraternity.

Zoe Tasia: Better Late than Never
Can you keep a promise after you die?

RJ Meldrum: The Coffin Express
A young man in Victorian London takes a new job with a railway company...one that carries the dead.

Krystal Garrett: Unleashed at the Terminal
Confronted with a demonic force, a former stay-at-home digs deep to find the courage she needs.

Joseph S Walker: Between the Ties
With their fathers away at war, two boys come across an abandoned railcar that simply shouldn't exist.

Arthur Conan Doyle: The Man with the Watches
Three passengers have disappeared, and a dead body is found. How could the vanished travellers leave the moving train, and how did the murdered man get on?

Cage Dunn: Blood Lake Train
A man, a memory, a sentient train – and blood spills on the tracks.

Michele Cacano: Seven Stations in Tokyo
Two people living in Tokyo choose the same day to face their ghosts;
one is haunted by her past, the other, by his future.

Karen Heard: Out of Order
A girl stuck in a train toilet fears what may be lurking on the other
side of the door. When the lights go out, the screaming starts.

Charles Dickens: The Signal-Man
Whenever the signal-man receives a warning from the spectre, a
terrible accident unfolds – and he is unable to prevent it.

AUTHOR'S COMMENTS ON THE STORY

The first time I added a paragraph about the inspiration for the story, readers reacted with enthusiasm and praised this concept in their customer reviews. Ever since, I've been using this idea, and it works well.

Here are three examples from my own collection, *The Bride's Curse: Bulgarian Gothic Ghost and Horror Stories.*

Author's Note (for the story 'Footsteps in the Snow')

Many rural houses in Bulgaria get abandoned because young people flock to cities and foreign countries to pursue careers. I often visit the deserted derelict buildings in my neighbourhood, where I hear my own footsteps crunch on concrete rubble and broken roof tiles. In some of these buildings I find broken furniture and other detritus of the people who once lived here, and even scraps of lace curtains still dangling in the shattered windows.

On one such visit, I asked myself: "What if…. I had to spend the night in one of those buildings? What might be the reason? How would I fare?"

But the story didn't really take shape until one cold February day, when I was trudging home through calf-deep snow. Someone had walked before me, leaving clear footprints which ended suddenly – outside an abandoned house. The person seemed to have walked right through the bricked-up door in the wall.

Author's Note (for the story 'The Bride's Curse')

I love visiting the old abandoned houses and soaking up their creepy romance. My black cat Sulu often comes with me. He enjoys exploring decayed spaces, balancing on charred timbers, picking his way across shattered tiles. But there was one house in the neighbourhood that Sulu resolutely refused to enter. His hair rose, his tail stood puffed up and rigid, his back arched. Perhaps he could sense something that I didn't?

The house was so beautiful, with great views over the hills and the cemetery, that I wondered why nobody had snatched it up. I visited repeatedly and marvelled at the furniture and suitcase left behind. Then I found out the house's history: the young woman buried alive, her curse and the documented ghastly deaths, and I wondered if my visits were wise. Perhaps I should have paid attention to Sulu's sixth sense?

I read an archive newspaper article about the last legal occupant's death – the body was really found dismembered in the freezer – and that article included excerpts from the investigating police officer's and the pathologist's reports.

Visiting, I had obviously not come to harm. Yet the many documented deaths of people soon after they moved in suggested there was something evil at work. I let my imagination run wild: What exactly was the nature of the curse?

This is how the tale started in my mind. I changed many details of the house's architecture and history, so it can't be identified.

I'm not frightened of visiting that house... but frankly, after learning its story, I would not want to live there, or even spend a single night.

Author's Note (for the story 'In the Gothic Chair')

During three cold, foggy November days, I stayed in Veliko Tarnovo, the ancient city that used to be Bulgaria's capital. I strolled along the narrow, slush-slippery lanes of the Old Town where mist wafted between historic buildings with overhanging upper storeys and painted façades. I browsed shop windows displaying folk costumes, souvenirs and classy handmade crafts. I particularly admired the artist-created ceramics, and wished I had enough time to choose a set of jewel-coloured cups.

For many years, I had toyed with the concept of a shop selling time, bottled in flagons, at an exorbitant price. Now I asked myself, "What if one of those Old Town shops officially displays antiques or souvenirs, but is covertly selling bottled time?"

As I allowed my imagination to wander, I saw in my mind not flagons but a strange, Gothic-style wooden chair. I tried to ignore it, but the image wouldn't go away. So I asked myself, "What is this creepy chair doing here?"

That's when the story idea took shape.

These notes don't need to be long. Two or three sentences often suffice. You can use the heading 'Author's Note' or 'About This Story', and I recommend placing this note after the tale. This way, readers can enjoy the story without bias or spoilers, and get the additional insights afterwards.

AUTHOR BIOS

In an anthology, it's a good idea to publish brief biographies of the authors. Three to five sentences are enough. You can either place them all together in the book's endmatter, or put each after the writer's story.

The mini bio should include what this author writes (e.g. 'sweet romance novels' or 'food and travel blogger'), where she lives (e.g.

'in a restored lighthouse on the English coast' or 'on a ranch in Idaho') and something about interests besides writing ('she has a black belt in jiu-jitsu' or 'he enjoys cooking and makes his own wine'.) Optional: include a detail relating to the book's theme (e.g. for an anthology about cats, mention 'servant to three demanding felines' or 'volunteers in a cat shelter'.) The tone can be quirky and whimsical.

Avoid including URLS for two reasons. Web addresses often change, as writers switch to different service providers, social media and email management services, and dead links annoy readers. Online bookselling platforms often refuse to accept books containing links to competing sites, and a single URL can get the book blocked from major sales channels.

Here are some author bios from my anthology *Among the Headstones: Creepy Tales from the Graveyard.*

Tylluan Penry is a solitary pagan witch and author who lives in the Rhondda Valley, S.E. Wales, UK. She has written and published dozens of articles, almost 30 books, mostly non-fiction on paganism, folklore, herblore, magic, runes and psychic self-defence (ghosts, poltergeists, vampires etc.). She lives in a very haunted house!

Priscilla Bettis writes disturbing stories. She lives in Virginia on a winding road that ends in a centuries-old graveyard. The graveyard and its surrounding woods hint at secrets that inspire her stories. Priscilla shares a home with her two-legged and four-legged family members.

William Meikle is a Scottish writer, now living in Canada, with over thirty novels published in the genre press and more than 300 short story credits in thirteen countries. He has books available from a variety of publishers including Dark Regions Press and Severed Press and his work has appeared in a large number of professional anthologies and magazines. He lives in Newfoundland with whales, bald eagles and icebergs for company. When he's not writing he drinks beer, plays guitar, and dreams of fortune and glory.

NOVICE MISTAKE TO AVOID

Don't clutter the teaser line with too much content. Keep it simple.

Don't accept author bios which are boastful in tone or read like advertisements.

PROFESSIONAL TIP

Ask the writers to provide the taglines, author's notes and bios for their stories. Give them several examples, so they can see what you're after.

ASSIGNMENT

Do you want teaser lines, notes about the story and author bios in your book?

CHAPTER 19

WRITING THE INTRODUCTION

Your book should have an introduction which places the stories in context, provides insights into the topic and whets the reader's appetite. Who writes this introduction? You, in your role as either the author of the collection or the editor of the anthology.

HOW LONG SHOULD AN INTRODUCTION BE?

People looking to buy a book will usually start by reading the free sample pages. If a lengthy introduction takes up those pages, readers won't get to experience the actual stories, and may be less likely to buy.

If an introduction is very short, it will feel superficial, and give the impression that the editor doesn't have much to say about the topic. Readers assume that the editor isn't very knowledgeable or doesn't care – and if they think the editor doesn't understand the subject or doesn't care, readers may not care either.

For a collection of my own stories, I aim for 200-400 words, and for an anthology, 350-750. You could have a shorter introduction if the book itself is very short. If the book is an anthology of literary classics or a 'Best of the Year…' genre compilation, the introduction may be longer, providing a thoughtful analysis of literary history or trends.

WHAT GOES IN THE INTRODUCTION?

While there are no rules, you may want to include the following:

- What kind of stories the book contains

- What kind of reading experience the reader can expect

- In the case of an anthology, how the stories were chosen

- Some insightful thoughts about the genre or theme

- The editor's personal connection to the theme

- Linguistic notes (e.g. American/British English)

CHOOSING THE VOICE FOR THE INTRODUCTION

Although the introduction is a work of non-fiction, use fiction writing techniques to make it vivid. Use the senses, let readers see images, hear sounds, smell scents.

Make it flow. Avoid stilted language, convoluted sentences, Passive Voice, legalistic-sounding disclaimers and bragging.

ADDING A FOREWORD

A foreword is similar to an introduction, but someone else writes it. This is usually a renowned author of the genre, a celebrity connected with the theme, or a recognised authority in the field.

You don't need a foreword for your book, but it can help with marketing. The celebrity's or subject expert's name serves as an endorsement.

You can pay the foreword writer – in which case I suggest you offer the same fee as you pay the authors – or you can seek a win/win scenario, where the foreword writer benefits in other ways. For example, other authors are often happy to contribute a foreword, because it provides exposure and another publication credit.

If you get a foreword, I recommend that you keep the introduction short. Place the foreword before the introduction.

EXAMPLES

Here are introductions I have written for three of my most recent books – a single-author collection and two anthologies. Observe my use of the senses, how I show my personal connection with the theme, and how I evoke the mood of the Gothic genre.

Introduction to *The Bride's Curse:*
Bulgarian Gothic Ghost and Horror Stories
(single author collection)

Welcome to Bulgaria, my adopted country in the south east of Europe, snow-blanketed mountains and sun-baked plains, a land of deep pine forests and fragrant rose plantations, studded with remnants of past eras – ancient Thracian and Roman, medieval, Ottoman and Communist.

Join me on a fictional journey to remote villages where you'll meet native Bulgarians, travellers and expatriates, demons and ghosts. I've blended my personal experiences with Bulgarian folklore and mythology, and let my imagination roam. All the events and characters are my inventions, yet they're steeped in Bulgarian myth and reality.

The tales in this book belong to the 'quiet' horror category – more creepy than gory, rich in atmosphere and suspense. Instead of throwing you into a whirl of violent action, I'll take you on a gentle visit to experience Bulgaria – the wealth of her nature, her economic poverty, her legends and traditions, her creepy abandoned homes and her timeless beauty – all from the safety of your armchair.

The stories are personal, arising from my perceptions and imagination. Still, I hope you'll gain a 'feel' for the country. After each story, I'll tell you a little about the genesis of that tale, the sources of my inspiration.

Bulgarian artist Savina Mantovska from Sofia has created beautiful illustrations, enriching each story with her vision.

Some of the tales are brief, others longer. I'm using British words, grammar, spelling and punctuation.

Come and join me under the grape arbour while the sinking sun streaks the mountains with crimson and purple. Sip a blood-red pomegranate juice or a fiery rakia, and enjoy my creepy tales.

Rayne

Introduction to Among the Headstones: Creepy Tales from the Graveyard (anthology)

Even as a child, I loved cemeteries with their shady quietude. I often visited the graveyard at the forest edge beyond our village to escape my siblings' noisy squabbles. Between the dense hedges of dark green yew, I found the silence my soul craved.

I spent afternoons walking among the graves, with few visitors in the vicinity other than the occasional black-clad, gnarled old lady with a battered watering can. My sandaled feet crunched on the gravel paths. I admired the affluent shiny headstones with gilt lettering, and pitied the poor who were afforded only a white wooden cross.

Reading the inscriptions, I allowed my imagination to fill in the gaps: how had this boy died at such a young age? Why was this man not joined by his widow, even though his text on his headstone had clearly left space for her name? Who was this girl who at eighteen had already left a grieving husband?

Many graves featured glass chalices filled with holy water, which on hot days gave off a faint scent of frankincense. Following German custom, I dipped a twig of yew into the bowls and splashed drops across the mounds, whispering a wish for the residents' eternal rest.

Some graves – especially the recent ones, still festooned in wreaths and ribbons – erupted in bursts of bright flowers, lovingly visited and tended every day. Others were planted with heather and creeping junipers, so they merely needed a trim once a year. Yet others remained uncared for, forgotten, overgrown with ivy and desiccated weeds.

I wondered: could the buried people see their graves? Did they know who came to visit and how often? Did they appreciate the floral offerings, or feel pained to be forgotten? What if they envied their better-served neighbours or resented the neglect?

In the silence of the cemetery, my mind found a fertile ground for wanderings. I did not realise it then, but those afternoons among the graves laid the foundation for my destiny as a writer of Gothic fiction.

I was curious to find out how the other writers perceived cemeteries, and what stories they wove around the graves. For this volume, I have collected twenty-seven of the finest – and creepiest – graveyard tales. The book features the works of established writers, classic authors and fresh voices.

Each contributor has a different writing voice and approach to story-telling, so you are bound to find tales you love. As you read, you may want to decide which story is your personal favourite.

The tales are set in different countries. We'll visit graveyards in Britain, Indonesia, Russia, China, Italy, Bulgaria, Thailand, USA, Australia, South Africa and Japan, and you can marvel at the burial customs of other cultures.

After each story, I've invited the authors to tell us where they got the idea from, revealing the source of their inspiration.

To preserve the authors' individual voices, I've left the differences between American and British English (and the Australian variant), and merely smoothed out linguistic bumps for writers whose main language is not English.

Now let's open the gate – can you hear it creak on its hinges? – and enter the realm of the dead. Listen to the wind rustling the yew, the grating of footsteps on gravel, the hoo-hoo-hoo of the collared dove.

Run your fingers across the tombstones to feel their lichen-rough sandstone or smooth cool marble. Inhale the scents of decaying lilies and freshly dug earth.

But be careful... someone may be watching your every movement... They may be right behind you.

Rayne Hall

Introduction to The Haunted Train: Creepy Tales from the Railways (anthology)

My father was a stationmaster, and for my first five years, I lived in an old railway station. Steam trains thundered past, huge black locomotives, their bellies bulging with fiery coals and dark menace.

During the day, trains halted right in front of our home, forcing me to endure their fearsome presence while they unloaded their heavy freight. The monsters breathed out clouds of black smoke and white steam, and no matter how hard I pressed my palms to my ears, their shrill whistles pierced my bones. I tried to flee, but there was nowhere to run.

Lying awake at night, with the duvet pulled over my face, I felt the trains rumble past. Wooden shutters rattled and brick walls trembled from their might. Although I knew I was safe, the steam engines terrified me out of my wits, and my imagination conjured up dangers. *I did not realise it then, but those fears were the departure point for my journey as a writer and editor of Gothic fiction.*

Yes, those trains scared me – yet they also intrigued me: the places they were coming from and going to, the strange passengers they carried, the mysterious containers they unloaded on the goods ramp.

To me, trains represent allure and danger, beauty and menace, the familiarity of the home and the terror of the unknown, a fierce power at the same time untameable and under control. Station buildings – whether historical and picturesque, functional and sturdy, or forgotten and decayed – symbolise both strength and vulnerability, both a shelter and a trap.

When I talked with other writers, I discovered that they shared my fascination with trains, and that their feelings, like mine, were rooted in intense personal memories.

In compiling this anthology, I have treated myself and my readers to journeys in different locations: a funicular railway in Victorian England, a freight train in the Carpathian Mountains, a high-tech sky train in Bangkok, an underground railway in Tokyo. We'll visit stations which lure with the promise of safe shelter but harbour unexpected dangers, meet the people who work on the tracks – stationmasters, porters, signalmen – and those who travel – commuters, tourists, dead bodies, murderers and ghosts.

In this volume, I have collected twenty of the finest – and creepiest – railway tales. The book features the works of established writers, classic authors and fresh voices. Each contributor has a different writing voice and approach to storytelling, so you are bound to find tales you love. As you read, you may want to decide which story is your personal favourite.

Some stories are spooky, some downright scary, while others pose a puzzling mystery. Some are short, some long. Some pose the question: what would you have done in the narrator's situation?

To preserve the authors' individual voices, I've left the differences between American and British English. After each story, I've invited the authors to tell us where they got the idea from, revealing the sources of their inspiration.

Are you prepared to come on board this train? Already, the steam engine is huffing in impatience. Listen to the chuff-chuff-chuff *from the locomotive and* tarattata-tarattata *of the giant wheels. Press your face against the dust-streaked window, inhale the smells of coal smoke and old textiles, watch the landscape whoosh past as you leave the familiar behind and journey into the unknown.*

But be careful: you can't know the train's real destination, nor your fellow travellers' intentions. Once you've closed that door behind you and the wheels start rolling, you may not be able to get out.

Rayne Hall

NOVICE MISTAKE TO AVOID

Don't bore readers with a lengthy, dull introduction. Otherwise they'll neither read on nor buy the book.

STRATEGY FOR SUCCESS

Try to match the voice of the introduction to the mood of the stories. Are the stories romantic and uplifting? Then your introduction should have the same romantic, uplifting feel. Do the tales inspire a sense of awe and wonder? Then seek to evoke awe and wonder in the introduction. Remember, this is the first piece of text readers get when they access the free sample pages. Let them taste the flavour of what's to come.

ASSIGNMENTS

1. Read the introductions to five anthologies, preferably in your project's genre. If you don't want to buy the books, you can access the introductions by clicking on the free sample offer.

2. Observe your reactions: what whets your interest in the stories, and what bores you?

3. If you were a book lover looking for an anthology to read, which of those five introductions would persuade you to hit the 'Buy Now' button?

4. Take notes about the approaches which work, and think about how you can adapt them for our own project.

CHAPTER 20

FRONTMATTER AND ENDMATTER

What goes before and after a book's main content is 'frontmatter' and 'endmatter'. Let's look at what goes in those sections.

IMPRINT

When you open a book, the first thing you normally see is the imprint page which contains basic publishing information, such as the title and subtitle, the name of the author (for a single-author collection) or of the editor in charge (for an anthology), the year of publication, and who owns the copyright.

In addition, the imprint page may contain information about the illustrator, the city where the book was printed, the edition, an ISBN number and brief disclaimers, if these elements are relevant.

Here's the imprint of one of my recent anthologies:

Headstones: Creepy Tales from the Graveyard

Edited by Rayne Hall

Copyright: ©2022 Rayne Hall
The individual stories are © the authors
Cover illustration and design by Savina Mantovska (© Rayne Hall)
(January 2022 Edition)

Please respect the copyright and do not publish or distribute any of these stories without permission from their authors. Unless otherwise stated, all characters are fictional and exist only in the authors' imagination, and any resemblance to people living or dead is coincidence.

TABLE OF CONTENTS

This is the list of stories. For a printed book, this shows the page number where the story starts. For an ebook, the table of contents contains clickable links which lead the reader directly to the stories.

In an anthology, the story list also includes the authors' names.

If you have created teaser lines for the stories, you can display them here. This is optional, but I recommend it because it entices readers.

The table of contents also lists the foreword, introduction, acknowledgements and other important elements.

FOREWORD AND INTRODUCTION

The previous chapter looks at these in detail. In the book's structure, the foreword comes before the introduction.

ACKNOWLEDGEMENTS

The book's author (or, in the case of an anthology, the book's editor) thanks the people who helped, e.g. sponsors, critiquers and beta-readers, the understanding husband. (I sometimes thank my cat Sulu who snuggled on the desk between my arms while I wrote.)

The acknowledgements page is also a good place to identify the professionals you hired who aren't mentioned in the imprint, e.g. the copyeditor, the proofreader, the formatter.

The acknowledgements page can be in the frontmatter or the endmatter.

AFTERWORD

This section is a message from the author of the collection (or the editor of the anthology) to the readers. You express your hope that they enjoyed the book, and suggest that they write and post a review. If you like, you can share additional information about the creative process, and you can provide an email address where they can contact you to point out typos and such.

I like to head this section 'Dear Reader' to make it more personal than 'Afterword', and I conclude it with my name.

AUTHOR BIO

Readers who've finished a book like to find out about the person who wrote it. Although an author bio is an optional element, I recommend including it. Under the heading 'About the Author' write a few sentences.

For an anthology, if you haven't placed the authors' bios under their stories, you can add a section 'About the Authors' in the endmatter.

PROMOTION FOR OTHER BOOKS

When readers have reached the end of a book they enjoyed, they're ready to buy another. At this stage, they're receptive to promotional messages. Tell them about other books in the series, or other works by the same author.

NOVICE MISTAKE TO AVOID

Don't clutter up the frontmatter with lengthy disclaimers, advertising messages, endorsements and unnecessary items. Readers want to get to the stories.

This is especially important for ebooks, because readers decide which book to buy based on the free sample. Since the free sample consists of the first few pages, those are valuable 'real estate'. If readers don't get to read at least part of a story, they won't be hooked, and will buy a different book instead.

STRATEGY FOR SUCCESS

Although the acknowledgements have traditionally been placed in the frontmatter, shift them to the endmatter. This way, they won't take up valuable sample page space.

ASSIGNMENT

Study the structure of several anthologies or single-author collections to see what is included in their frontmatter and endmatter.

CHAPTER 21

THE BOOK COVER AND ILLUSTRATIONS

Your book needs a great cover to catch the eye and attract the attention of potential buyers. Drawings which illustrate the stories can act as an additional pull.

WHAT GOES ON THE COVER?

- First, choose a picture. This can be a good quality photo you have taken, a painting created by an artist or a free or purchased stock image. It needs to convey both the theme and the genre at a glance. Make sure you have the copyright holder's permission to use the picture: you can't just take an image from the internet

- The book's title. This is in a large, bold font

- The subtitle

- The author's name (e.g. 'Suzie Scrybe' for a single-author collection) or the editor's name prefaced with 'edited by' (e.g. 'edited by Eddie Torr' for an anthology)

Since most books are sold online, the cover needs to look good when viewed at thumbnail size. Simplicity with just a few elements works better than a complicated, cluttered design.

If your budget permits, you can hire a designer to create a professional cover. However, the leading self-publishing platforms offer free apps and templates which allow you to create a stunning cover with just a few clicks.

WHAT GOES ON THE BACK COVER?

Only printed books have back covers, ebooks don't.

The back features a description of the book, introducing the genre and theme. You may be able to repurpose a few sentences from the introduction. If you like, you can also list the names of all the authors and illustrators who contributed to the anthology.

STORY ILLUSTRATIONS

Do you need illustrations? No. But in some circumstances, they can enhance the book's appeal.

For example, if your book has a local theme and is sold mostly in physical locations (bookshops, art fairs), potential customers flicking through the pages will recognise local scenes, pause and smile… and are more likely to buy.

When I wrote my collection *The Bride's Curse: Bulgarian Gothic Ghost and Horror Stories,* I set the stories in Bulgaria, the country where I live. To prospective readers who don't know me, my German nationality and English-sounding pen-name wouldn't signal 'authentic Bulgarian content'. My solution: I hired a Bulgarian artist – Savina Mantovska – to illustrate the stories. When viewers see the book online, they see a Bulgarian name, and when they flick through the pages, they see typical Bulgarian images.

If you decide to get illustrations, one picture per story works well.

Where do you find artists? If you have a large enough budget, hire a professional illustrator who understands the requirements. Otherwise, you can ask a friend with artistic skills, and perhaps barter services.

Art students, as well as amateurs transitioning from hobby to career, are often happy to create illustrations for token payments. They appreciate the opportunity to gain practical experience in commissioned work, to build their list of published works, and to enrich their portfolio with attractive samples they can show to future clients. However, keep in mind that inexperienced artists don't have the same skills as professionals. They don't yet know what works and what doesn't, and depend on guidance from you. A first-time book publisher working with a novice illustrator can be a case of the blind leading the blind.

The illustrations need to look attractive, and need to reproduce well in print and not increase the file size and digital delivery costs. Unless you're working with a professional illustrator, I recommend that you ask for line drawings with bold black lines on a white background.

NOVICE MISTAKES TO AVOID

Don't clutter up the front cover. The more text elements and pictures the cover contains, the less power it has to grab the attention at first glance.

These days, most books are sold online, so the cover has to work above all when displayed at thumbnail size on a page among many other covers, so simplicity is crucial. I advise against endorsements, slogans, advertisements, contributors' names and additional pictures. Those can go on the paperback's back cover.

STRATEGY FOR SUCCESS

If this book is successful, you may want to publish more books of the same kind, so choose a design which can be replicated for a series, changing just the image and title.

ASSIGNMENT

Study the book covers of several books similar to your project – e.g. collections and anthologies of the same genre or with related themes – especially the bestselling ones. What do the covers contain? What design elements do they have in common?

CHAPTER 22

THE PUBLICATION PROCESS

When your book is as good as you can make it, edited and proofread, it's time for publication. Major self-publishing platforms offer all the tools you need, and they're free to use. You need computer skills, the ability to follow online instructions, time and patience.

FORMATTING

In this process, you take the manuscript and shape it to look like a real book, with consistent fonts for headings, bylines, teasers and body text, table of contents, page numbers, illustrations and more. Formatting a book requires skill, so if you are inexperienced in this field, I recommend getting help. You can hire a formatter or barter services.

All other steps are relatively easy, and you should be able to complete the following without help.

UPLOADING

Simply upload the formatted book and the book cover on your chosen self-publishing platform, e.g. Amazon or Draft2Digital. This will take just a few clicks, though the process can take several minutes.

(If you don't have a formatted manuscript or a designed cover yet, many platforms offer apps for doing it yourself, with just an unformatted manuscript and a picture.)

BOOK DESCRIPTION

You will be asked to write a book description, the so-called 'blurb'. This is your main sales tool, so spend time crafting it. You may be able to repurpose some paragraphs from your introduction.

I suggest including a list of the stories in the collection, complete with author names (for anthologies) and teaser lines.

META DATA

This is the information the bookselling site will use to position and market the book. The most important of these is the genre (or 'category'). Different sites use different category systems, and this can make the search for the right genre a frustrating experience.

Some publishing platforms allow you to choose seven or ten different categories, others permit only one or two. Tick as many as you are allowed, because more genres bring more exposure and more sales.

If you have to choose between several categories, pick the most specialised one, because that's where your book has a chance to stand out. So, instead of the broad genre 'Fantasy' select 'Urban Fantasy' or better still, 'Urban Fantasy – Short Story Collections'. Instead of 'Anthologies' select 'Anthologies – Fiction – Historical'.

Another crucial piece of meta data is the keywords. These are the words for the bookselling site's search engine. The more keywords you provide, the more often your book will show up when readers search the site for their next read. Use the 'long tail' strategy for choosing keywords, that is, specialised rather than general. 'Funny Love Stories' is better than 'Love', and 'Gothic Horror Anthology' is better than 'Horror'.

You will also get the opportunity to list the contributors. Include as many authors' names as the publishing platform permits. This is a great marketing advantage because of the way bookselling sites' algorithms work. The more books an author has, and the more copies that book sells, the more exposure the authors' other books get. Your anthology will benefit from all the contributors' sales successes – and in return, the contributors' books benefit from the anthology.

Unfortunately, some publishing platforms allow only a limited number of contributors – not enough to cover everyone who has a story in the anthology. Which names should you include in the meta data? First, the editor in charge, second, the well-known foreword writer if you have one. Fill the remaining spots with authors who currently have books published, because this yields the greatest benefits for their books and yours. To avoid hurt feelings, include every author's name in the book description.

EBOOKS AND PAPERBACKS

Most anthologies and single-author collections are worth publishing both in paperback and as ebooks. Ebooks are easiest, paperbacks require more effort.

For paperbacks, the modern print-on-demand method usually works best. The book doesn't get printed until a customer has ordered and paid for it. Then a single copy gets printed and sent directly to the customer. The publishing platform and the bookseller take everything; you simply receive the money (minus the costs and commissions). This approach means you have very little work, and you don't need to invest money upfront or maintain warehousing space for unsold copies. Print-on-demand is the method I recommend for most books and anthologies.

However, if you have a local theme and expect to sell mostly physical copies in your locality (for example a writers' group's anthology), then the old-fashioned approach of ordering a large number of printed books may be better. For this, you will need to invest money upfront (to pay for the full print run of several hundred or several thousand copies), as well as transport facilities and storage space. The production costs per copy are lower, so you can sell the books cheaper, and by using a local printing company, you can build local goodwill.

Other formats – e.g. audiobooks – are more complicated to produce and may require a major investment of time and money. I suggest that you launch the book in paperback and ebook first, and if it sells well, follow this up with an audio edition.

PRICING

To decide on the book's price, look at what other recently published books of the same type cost, and use this as a guide. As a relatively unknown writer, you should probably charge less than that genre's bestselling author, but don't try to make your book cheaper than everyone else's, because that strategy doesn't work.

If you change your mind about the price later, you can lower or increase it with a few clicks.

NOVICE MISTAKE TO AVOID

Don't skimp on the meta data. In a hurry to get the book published, you may be tempted to leave out inessential information, to pick random categories or to write a slapdash book description. Don't. What you insert here is your main marketing tool, and it's free.

STRATEGY FOR SUCCESS

Consider giving your book a very low sales price for pre-publication orders and during the launch week. Announce this special offer, and say that after a certain date, the price will go up. This motivates people to buy or order the book while the offer is on. The large number of sales during the launch can help the book climb in the sales charts, and this in turn generates more exposure which then leads to more sales in the future.

ASSIGNMENT

Imagine readers looking to buy a book like yours. What words or phrases will they type into the search box?

CHAPTER 23

PUBLICITY AND MARKETING

You have created a great book: now how do you find readers and purchasers for it?

The key to successful marketing is to reach out to the kind of people who typically read this kind of book.

With an anthology, you can multiply your marketing by involving the contributors. In this chapter, I'll show you how.

PROMOTING BOOKS ON BLOGS

Get the book featured in an interesting way on blogs which have a similar target audience. This reaches the right readers and costs you nothing – though it requires thought and time.

Most bloggers struggle to fill their blogs with informative, entertaining material, so they will welcome contributions they can just slot in. The trick is to offer the bloggers ready-made, high-quality content, tailored to their audience.

Your strategy should be to create high-value content – not just excerpts and dull promotional texts. This requires work, but it's a good investment. It's better to spend time on creating high-quality material for high-quality posts than to churn out masses of boring promo texts for blogs which nobody reads.

The best promotions are those which don't look like promotions, but entice readers with information and entertainment.

HOW TO IDENTIFY THE BEST BLOGS TO GUEST ON

How can you tell if a blog is worth spending time on? Here are the criteria.

- The blog focuses either on the book's genre or the book's theme. Let's say your anthology contains tales of shipboard romance – love stories set on cruise liners, ferries, freighters and yachts. Then you look for blogs dedicated to Romance fiction, and also blogs about cruises, sailing and travel

- The blog is active. Posts are frequent and more or less regular, perhaps once a week. Don't bother with dead and comatose blogs where no post has appeared for over a year

- The blog has quality content. Are the posts thoughtful, informative, entertaining, stimulating? Do you find it worthwhile reading them? Then this is a blog worth contributing to. If you just glance at the posts and don't see anything worth reading, then other people won't spend their time on it either

- The blog gets read. An easy way to assess this is the number and content of the comments. Do blog readers post questions and opinions under each post? That's a good sign

- Metrics (calculated by apps to determine the blog's site authority, number of visitors, average time spent, popularity and such) can be useful – but those are often artificially inflated (e.g. by paid-for fake clicks), so they don't necessarily reflect the true picture

- Consider a swap with other authors or editors of the genre: They publish a guest post written by you, and you host one written by them on your blog. Since you both have largely the same target audience, everyone benefits from this arrangement

- Don't pay for a 'blog tour' which promises to book you guest slots on grand blogs and even obtain book reviews. In practice, these don't bring your book the kind of publicity it needs, because the 'tour stops' are blogs filled with boring promotions which nobody ever reads. The only one who benefits is the person who sold you the tour

WHAT DO BLOGGERS WANT?

Bloggers – the kind worth targeting – want to save time, and they want quality material. Help them by offering well-written, interesting posts, exactly right for their target audience.

These can be guest posts written by you or the contributors, interviews, or 'round-up' articles. We'll look at each of these in a moment.

I suggest you start by studying the blogs carefully, reading several articles to get a feel for them. Leave comments on some recent posts. This will bring you to the bloggers' attention in a positive way, so they'll recognise your name when you approach them.

Next, send them a message – probably through the blog's 'Contact' function, offering a specific article (or choice of articles). These should be articles you or a contributor have already written, or are willing to write.

Can you provide illustrations? Then say so. Most bloggers prefer posts with one or several images. Photos taken by the author are especially welcome.

GUEST POSTS

Write articles which are of interest to readers of both your book and the blog. Also encourage the contributing authors to write articles. Some of them will be happy to, because it gives them additional exposure and provides publicity for their own books.

The best topics are related to the book's genre and theme. Here are some examples from my own books.

For my single-author collection *The Bride's Curse: Bulgarian Gothic Ghost and Horror Stories,* I wrote an article about the reasons why so many houses in Bulgaria get abandoned and fall into ruin, and one about a cursed house in my neighbourhood where several gruesome murders were committed.

For the anthology *Among the Headstones: Creepy Tales from the Graveyard,* author Lee Morgan wrote about the historical practice of bodysnatching (digging up corpses for scientific dissection), Morgan Pryce described funeral traditions in Thailand, and Tylluan Penry shared childhood memories of growing up in a haunted home.

I matched each of these articles with the blog for which it was the best fit. You can do the same.

End every article with a question to encourage comments. "Have you ever seen a ghost? What would you do if you encountered one? Tell us about it in the Comments below." This stimulates engagement, which bloggers value, and gives the post more visibility.

PROVIDE READY-WRITTEN INTERVIEWS

Interview the contributors (or simply yourself) and offer the ready-written interviews to bloggers.

The strategy here is to ask the kind of questions the readers of that blog would want to ask. For example, if you seek to promote an anthology of love stories for a Romance fiction blog, you would ask questions like, "What's the most romantic place you've been to?" "What's your idea of a perfect date?" "How did your husband propose to you?" For my Gothic Horror anthologies, I ask my writers, "Have you ever seen a ghost?" "What's the creepiest place you've been to?" "What were you afraid of as a child?"

I suggest you compile about thirty questions, and allow the writers to choose which ones to answer and which to leave out. Encourage them to provide as many answers as possible, and to use their writing skills to get the tone of the genre (for example, joyful and tender for a Romance anthology, atmospheric and creepy for a Gothic book).

The typical interview will cover five to ten questions, so if an author provides twenty answers, these will yield material for three interviews. If twenty authors participate, you'll have around sixty interviews which you can place on blogs. That's a lot of highly targeted, free publicity. Choose the questions and answers which suit the blog best.

ROUND-UP ARTICLES

These work well for anthologies. If several authors provided interesting answers to a question, combine their replies to form an article.

'Twelve Romance Writers Remember their Most Romantic Dates' – 'Four Romance Authors Confess Their Love Secrets' – 'Romance Authors Reveal How Their Spouses Proposed' and so on.

For my Gothic Horror anthologies, I've created several round-up articles, such as 'Have You Ever Met a Ghost? Horror Writers Talk About Real-Life Spooky Encounters' – 'Gothic Horror Authors Share Their Scariest Train Journeys' – 'Ten Horror Authors Reveal Their Secret Fears' – 'Gothic Horror Writers Show us the Creepiest Places They've Ever Seen' and more.

You can use the individual answers twice – in a round-up article as well as in an interview. The posts will be very different, with just one repeated paragraph.

HOW TO USE BLOG POSTS TO PROMOTE THE BOOK

At the end of the article, add the following elements:

- a short bio of the guest post's author or the interviewee, perhaps including a sales link to one of their own books, as well as a headshot photo

- a description of the book, including a sales link

- the book's cover

Bloggers are normally happy to include these elements. Often, they earn a small commission from the bookselling site whenever a reader clicks on the link and buys the book. This is a win/win arrangement.

PROMOTING THE BLOG POSTS

The more comments a post receives, the higher it ranks within that blog (and, depending on the blog platform, also in internet search engines). Comment on the posts you have written, and reply whenever someone else leaves a comment.

With anthologies, mobilise all the contributors. Even those who chose not to write guest posts can comment on the other authors' posts. This will quickly catapult the article into the list of most popular posts on the blog and lead to increased visibility.

Use social media to promote the blog posts, and encourage the contributors to do the same on whatever social media platform they use. More about this in the next section.

SOCIAL MEDIA

In the social media, you can promote the book as well as the articles which promote the book. Encourage the contributors to do the same.

A personal slant works best. For example, "I have a story in this book, my first ever published piece!" or "My story 'The Mine Shaft' has been reprinted in this Horror anthology. It's the scariest story I've ever written – I scared myself writing it." "Here's an article I wrote about shipboard romances."

Different contributors will use different social media, so the book (or the articles) will get wide exposure. Encourage other contributors who use the same platforms to like, share and, above all, reply with questions to start discussions.

Social media posts gain more attention if they have eye-catching pictures, so you may want to give your contributors ready-made images. Since most platforms use horizontal rather than vertical images, book covers alone don't work well. However, you can place the book cover on an atmospheric horizontal background which conveys the genre. For example, a Gothic Mystery anthology could feature the book cover on a background of swirling mist.

If the book has illustrations, those may be useable for social media posts.

NOVICE MISTAKE TO AVOID

Don't spend money on paid promotions and advertisements in the expectation that these will accelerate sales and bring a big return on investment. Ads and paid promos rarely lead to increased sales, and are usually money flushed down the toilet.

People these days don't pay attention to advertising messages. They're so inundated with promotional messages that they simply tune it all out.

If you have the budget to invest in advertising and paid promotions, and want to try this, focus on the places where the target audience hang out. For example, to promote your collection of Paranormal Romance stories, advertise on sites devoted to Paranormal Romance fiction.

NOVICE MISTAKE TO AVOID

Don't spend money or time on blogs which contain nothing but promotional posts, because those don't get read by anyone.

STRATEGY FOR SUCCESS

You can recycle the articles you've written, and get them published on several blogs. It's considered courteous to wait a year before offering the article to someone else.

If anthology contributors wrote articles, they can adapt them as guest blogs in the future to promote their own books, or publish them on their own websites.

ASSIGNMENTS

1. Identify at least five desirable blogs.

2. Make a list of at least ten guest blog topic ideas related to your book's theme or genre.

CHAPTER 24

GETTING REVIEWS FOR YOUR BOOK

Reviews by genuine readers are the Number One promotional tool – but they're not easy to get. Genuine reviews can't be purchased, swapped, bribed, faked or forced. You can, however, entice them.

TIPS FOR HOW TO GET READER REVIEWS FOR YOUR BOOK

- The most useful reviews are those posted on bookselling sites, because that's where people buy their next book. Also useful are reviews on sites for booklovers, and genre-specific book blogs

- Contact book reviewers who specialise in the genre and post their assessments on their genre blogs. Keep in mind that most book reviewers get inundated with review requests and may not be able to take on your book

- Start courting book reviewers before the book is published. Offer them ARCs, that is, advance review copies

- Ask friends. Keep in mind that although they like you, they may not like the book, which can put them in an awkward situation. Assure them that they don't need to read and review the book if it's 'not their thing', and that they don't need to pretend to like it

- Suggest to reviewers that they mention which is their favourite story, and why. The variety of tastes is amazing to see – just about every story will be someone's top favourite – and the reviews will add up to give a comprehensive, positive view of the book

- Book reviewers get the book free, but they don't get anything else – no money, no gifts, no sweepstake tickets

- Most reviewers accept ebooks, but some insist on paperbacks. The cost of paperbacks for reviewers is usually a good investment

INVOLVE THE CONTRIBUTORS

If your book is an anthology, enlist the help of the contributors. They're not allowed to review the book themselves – that's against the rules of practically every site – but they can ask their friends and fans. If twenty writers have stories in the book, and each persuades on average two people, that's forty reviews.

WHAT IF THE BOOK GETS NEGATIVE REVIEWS?

Don't worry if a reviewer dislikes the book: this just shows that different people have different tastes. If the critical reviewers explain what they dislike, this may actually entice readers who seek exactly what those reviewers disdained. For example, "These Romance stories lacked sexual action" will attract readers who prefer 'clean' fiction.

You may also get crank reviews from people who haven't even read the book and simply vent their negativity, for example, disgruntled writers who resent that their story hasn't been included. Ignore them.

NOVICE MISTAKE TO AVOID

Don't pay for customer reviews. That's against the rule of every bookselling and book-reviewing site, and can get you and your book banned.

Don't swap reviews with other authors and editors. Not only is this against the rules, but it leads to ethical dilemmas and ill will if one doesn't like the other's book.

STRATEGY FOR SUCCESS

At the end of the book, put a 'Dear Reader' message, suggesting a review. These people have already invested the reading time, and they have formed an opinion, so now need to spend just a few minutes to type up their thoughts. This is the most effective method, it costs nothing, and the reviews will be genuine.

ASSIGNMENT

Identify at least three ways in which you will seek to get reviews for your book.

DEAR READER,

I hope you found these tips helpful, and that you are brimming with inspiration, ideas and practical plans for your book.

You could really help me by writing a review about this book and posting it on a bookselling website, or perhaps in an online book-reading group, your social media or your blog. Feel free to mention the kind of story collection you're planning or working on (or have already published), and explain which chapters you found most helpful and why.

Email me the link to your review, and I'll send you a free review copy (ebook) of one of my other Writer's Craft books. Let me know which one you would like. There are around forty to choose from, so you can pick the one which will be most helpful at this stage of your journey as a writer. (For a title list with brief descriptions, see this page on my website. www.raynehall.com/books-for-writers.)

My email is contact@raynehall.com. Drop me a line if you've spotted any typos which have escaped the proofreader's eagle eyes, or want to give me private feedback or have questions.

You can also contact me through my social media accounts. I'm currently active on Instagram instagram.com/rayne_hall_author/, Mastodon https://writing.exchange/@Rayne_Hall_Author and Facebook https://www.facebook.com/RayneHallAuthor. If you contact me on one of those platforms to tell me that you've read this book, I'll probably follow you back.

If you want to hear from me more often, I have a newsletter/blog with writing tips, mini writing contests, special offers, information about upcoming books, and glimpses into my life in Bulgaria and adventures with my rescue cats. https://rayne.substack.com . Subscribers get a free pdf ebook, *Grow Your Author Voice.*

If you find this book helpful, it would be great if you could spread the word about it. Maybe you know other writers who would benefit.

I'm also adding an excerpt from another Writer's Craft Guide you may find useful: *Writing and Publishing Short Stories: Professional Techniques for Fiction Authors.* I hope you like it.

With best wishes for your writing success,

Rayne Hall

ACKNOWLEDGEMENTS

I give sincere thanks to writers K.D. Gearhart, Cage Dunn, CeeCee Claire, CT Bridges, Frank Parker, Lena Klassen, Marina Costa, Heidi Hunter, Deborah Edwards, Alyson Sheldrake and Ellie Rhodes who read the draft chapters and offered valuable feedback.

The cover is by Erica Syverson and Manuel Berbin. Julia Gibbs proofread the manuscript, and Eled Cernik formatted the book.

And finally, I say thank you to my sweet rescue cats Sulu and Uhura (Yura), who took turns snuggling on the desk between my arms while I typed, while McCoy and new kitten Chekhov tried to distract me.

Rayne Hall

SAMPLE CHAPTER FROM
WRITING AND PUBLISHING SHORT STORIES

Chapter 2

ARTIST BRAIN AND EDITOR BRAIN: CREATIVE AND CRITICAL PROCESSES

When you write, it's as if there are two different personalities working in your head – an artist and an editor.

I call them Artist Brain and Editor Brain.

Artist Brain excels at creative challenges, problem solving, playfulness, coming up with ideas, freewriting, brainstorming, originality, first drafts, spontaneous plotting, creating new stories... all of which are crucial for writers.

Editor Brain is good for analytical thinking, critical assessments, structuring plots, revising, editing, finding and correcting errors, tightening, business matters, formatting ... also crucial for writers.

Traditionally, it has been said that the left half of the human brain is analytical, and the right half creative. Although few modern scientists still subscribe to this model, you can use it to visualise the differences. Imagine Editor Brain living in the left half and Artist Brain in the right.

To create a great short story, we employ both – but at different times. Coming up with ideas and writing first drafts is a job for Artist Brain. Structuring the story and revising it is a job for Editor Brain.

Ideally, the two work together as colleagues, each doing what it's best at. In practice, the cooperation isn't always so smooth.

Editor Brain is often the assertive, jealous type, and sometimes it's a real bully. It can't bear to stand back and let Artist Brain get on with something. It interferes and censors, and tries to sabotage whatever Artist Brain does. It says things like, "This is crap." "This will never work." "This can't be done." "Hopeless." "Give up writing."

Artist Brain is the shy, sensitive type, easily intimidated, and freezes into inactivity when bullied. This can lead to a lack of creativity, dull prose, or writer's block.

Astonishingly, Artist Brain performs best under pressure and loves deadlines, the tighter, the better. That's why many writers find that timed writing challenges, contests with deadlines and writing marathons get their creative juices flowing. Given an impossibly tight deadline, you may produce your best-ever story.

Editor Brain, however, prefers time to carry out a job with slow, meticulous attention.

HOW TO ENCOURAGE YOUR ARTIST BRAIN

If your Artist Brain is cowering in the corner, here are four techniques for coaxing it into action:

- Use your non-dominant hand to do things for a few minutes (e.g. if you're right-handed, brush your teeth with your left hand). Many people find that this stimulates Artist Brain to become more active.

- Do some doodling, preferably in bright colours and in curvy lines. Artist Brain loves bright colours, circles, curves, and randomness. (Editor Brain prefers order, purpose, squares, straight lines, and black on white). Many writers find that a few minutes of doodling releases a pent-up creativity.

- Draw 'mind maps' using free associations, circles, curvy lines and coloured pens.

- Participate in short story writing contests with tight deadlines to give Artist Brain the chance to flourish under pressure.

This chapter, and the next one, are jobs for Artist Brain. Tell your Editor Brain to take a vacation so that Artist Brain can work undisturbed.

Editor Brain will have a starring role in some of the later chapters.

FUN WITH TITLES

For this assignment, you'll use Artist Brain. Artist Brain loves handwriting and colours, so you may want to do the exercise on paper with coloured pens. On the other hand, you may prefer to write it on your computer, since it saves typing it up afterwards. Maybe you can set your computer to use coloured fonts.

Get a kitchen timer or similar and set it for ten minutes.

During this time, write a list of title ideas. Just story titles, nothing else. Use your idea lists in Chapter 1 for inspiration, but don't feel restricted. If something comes to your mind, write it down, without censoring it. (Editor Brain may try to censor. Tell it to shut up.)

Ideas for story titles will probably come very fast. For example, if your list of settings includes modern day Shanghai, and the other lists include dragons, love and revenge, you can create titles like this:

- Dragons

- The Dragon

- Dragons in Love

- The Dragon's Revenge

- The Third Dragon

- Love of a Dragon

- The Dragon's Lover

- Vengeance

- The Dragon's Egg

- The Dragon's Nest

- The Dragon's Mate

- Three Dragons

- To Love a Dragon

- The Revenge

- A Lover's Revenge

- A Lover's Vengeance

- The Vengeful Lover

- The Dragon's Daughter

- The Vengeful Dragon

- Dragons in Shanghai

- Vengeance in Shanghai

- The Dragon of Shanghai

- Shanghai Dragons

- Shanghai Love

- The Dragon's Daughter

- My Daughter in Shanghai

- My Mother's Vengeance

- The Gambler of Shanghai

- and so on.

Keep going for ten minutes. In this time, you'll get a long, long list.

You can continue another time, adding yet more titles. Indeed, you may find ideas for titles flowing into your head while you take a shower or wash the dishes.

NOVICE MISTAKE TO AVOID

Don't let Editor Brain interfere with Artist Brain's work. Editor Brain's critical, disapproving attitude can stifle your creativity, kill the fun or cause writer's block.

PROFESSIONAL TIP

Imagine Artist Brain and Editor Brain as separate creatures – your employees, or perhaps as team members. Treat both with respect, and set each to work on the areas they're best at. If one tries to interfere with the other's work, say firmly, "This is not your job. I have important work for you later." I find this helps a lot.

ASSIGNMENT

After compiling the titles, take a short break. Make yourself a cup of coffee, drink a healthy glass of water, pet your cat, do some stretches or light aerobic exercise. Now look at the list of titles with fresh eyes. Keeping your mind still in Artist Brain mode, highlight the titles which pique your interest, the ones which would get your attention and curiosity if you saw them in a short story anthology. Highlight them, preferably with a bright colour.

BOOKS IN THE WRITER'S CRAFT SERIES

You can read them in any order. Which of them would be most helpful for your current writing project?

Writing Fight Scenes

Writing Scary Scenes

The Word-Loss Diet

Writing About Magic

Writing About Villains

Writing Dark Stories

Euphonics For Writers

Writing Short Stories to Promote Your Novels

Twitter for Writers

Why Does My Book Not Sell? 20 Simple Fixes, Writing Vivid Settings

How To Train Your Cat To Promote Your Book

Writing Deep Point of View

Getting Book Reviews

Novel Revision Prompts

Writing Vivid Dialogue

Writing Vivid Characters

Writing Book Blurbs and Synopses

Writing Vivid Plots

Write Your Way Out Of Depression: Practical Self-Therapy For Creative Writers

Fantasy Writing Prompts

Horror Writing Prompts

How to Write That Scene

More Horror Writing Prompts

Writing Love Scenes

Author Branding

Fiction Pacing

Ghostwriting

Writing Gothic Fiction

Fiction Pacing

Copywriting

Writing Romance Novels and Love Stories

Writing and Publishing a Book Series

Writing and Publishing Short Stories

… and more